OVERCOMING
Spiritual
Ailments
A 15-Week Study Guide

OVERCOMING

Spiritual

Ailments

A 15-Week Study Guide

BROOKLYN HECTOR

CITI OF
BOOKS

CITIOFBOOKS, INC.
3736 Eubank NE Suite A1
Albuquerque, NM 87111-3579
www.citiofbooks.com
Hotline: 1 (877) 389-2759
Fax: 1 (505) 930-7244

Ordering Information:
Quantity sales. Special discounts are available on quantity purchases by corporations, associations, and others. For details, contact the publisher at the address above.

Printed in the United States of America.

ISBN-13:	Softcover	979-8-89391-488-7
	eBook	979-8-89391-489-4

Library of Congress Control Number: 2024926523

Acknowledgment

First and foremost, I must thank **God**—not just for giving me the idea for this book but for not letting me ignore it! He kept nudging me, reminding me, and, let's be honest, probably shaking His head every time I tried to push it aside. But He made sure I kept coming back to the question: *Why do we feel the way we feel?* And here we are!

To my amazing husband, **Charles**—thank you for always putting up with me, encouraging me, and pushing me forward even when I wanted to throw in the towel (or at least take a long break). Your patience, love, and unwavering belief in me mean everything.

And to everyone reading this, you are the reason this book exists. I pray it blesses you, challenges you, and helps you see that sometimes, what we're feeling isn't just in our minds—it's in our spirit. Let's heal, grow, and walk this journey together!

--Brooklyn

Table of Contents

Welcome to our 15-week study guide on spiritual ailments. Throughout this journey, we will explore various spiritual challenges that believers often encounter. Each week, we will focus on a specific ailment, examining its impact on our spiritual lives and discovering biblical guidance to overcome it. Our goal is to deepen our relationship with God, find healing and strength in His Word, and grow in our spiritual walk.

Together, we will delve into the following topics:

Week 1: Spiritual Despair

Week 2: Spiritual Emptiness

Week 3: Spiritual Isolation

Week 4: Spiritual Guilt

Week 5: Spiritual Pride

Week 6: Spiritual Confusion

Week 7: Spiritual Anger

Week 8: Spiritual Fatigue

Week 9: Spiritual Envy

Week 10: Spiritual Attachment

Week 11: Spiritual Apathy

Week 12: Spiritual Doubt

Week 13: Spiritual Distress

Week 14: Spiritual Depression

Week 15: Spiritual Malnutrition

As we embark on this journey, let us commit to being open and honest with ourselves and God. Let's support each other in prayer and fellowship, seeking transformation and renewal in our spiritual lives.

Week 1: Spiritual Despair

Introduction:

Spiritual despair is a profound sense of loss, where one feels disconnected from their faith and spiritual beliefs. This condition can be deeply troubling, but the Bible provides guidance, comfort, and hope for those experiencing such a spiritual crisis.

Definition:

Spiritual Despair: Feeling a loss of faith or connection to one's spiritual beliefs.

Key Scriptures:

Psalm 42:11 (NIV) - "Why, my soul, are you downcast? Why so disturbed within me? Put your hope in God, for I will yet praise him, my Savior and my God."

Psalm 34:18 (NIV) - "The Lord is close to the brokenhearted and saves those who are crushed in spirit."

Isaiah 41:10 (NIV) - "So do not fear, for I am with you; do not be dismayed, for I am your God. I will strengthen you and help you; I will uphold you with my righteous right hand."

Matthew 11:28-30 (NIV) - "Come to me, all you who are weary and burdened, and I will give you rest..."

2 Corinthians 1:3-4 (NIV) - "Praise be to the God and Father of our Lord Jesus Christ, the Father of compassion and the God of all comfort..."

Monday: Acknowledging Despair and Finding Hope

Explanation of the Topic: Psalm 42:11 reminds us that it's okay to feel downcast and disturbed. Acknowledging our emotions is the first step towards healing. By putting our hope in God, we shift our focus from our troubles to His promises, finding strength and encouragement in His presence.

Discussion Question: Reflect on Psalm 42:11, which says, "Why, my soul, are you downcast? Why so disturbed within me? Put your hope in God, for I will yet praise him, my Savior and my God." Think deeply about the emotions expressed here. How does openly recognizing and acknowledging your feelings of despair help you confront what's weighing on your heart? When you shift from focusing solely on your struggles to placing your hope in God, how does this change the way you view your circumstances? Consider the moments when hope felt distant—how might actively choosing to trust in God's presence and promises bring peace or strength to your outlook, even in times of distress?

Real-World Example: Imagine someone, Alex, navigating a challenging period at work. Every day feels like an uphill battle as they deal with mounting responsibilities, lack of recognition, and constant pressure from management. They pour their heart into each task, but despite their dedication, they feel unseen and undervalued. Reaching a breaking point, Alex confides in a trusted colleague, sharing their frustrations and feelings of inadequacy. In response, the colleague listens empathetically, acknowledging Alex's struggles and encouraging them to search for moments of positivity and growth. They remind Alex to have faith in the journey, believing that resilience and trust in better days will eventually lead to renewal and change. This support gives Alex a small sense of hope, though the path forward still feels uncertain.

Small Prayer: Heavenly Father, I feel overwhelmed and downcast, but I choose to put my hope in You. Help me to trust in Your salvation and find peace in Your presence. Amen.

Tuesday: Reassurance in God's Presence

Explanation of the Topic: Psalm 34:18 reassures us that God is near to the brokenhearted and those in despair. Even in our lowest moments,

His presence offers comfort and salvation. Knowing that God is close can bring immense peace and hope.

Discussion Question: Psalm 34:18 says, "The Lord is close to the brokenhearted and saves those who are crushed in spirit." Reflect on the meaning of this verse. How does knowing that God is close to those who are hurting provide comfort during times of spiritual despair? Think about moments when you've felt alone or disconnected—how might this verse offer reassurance that God sees your struggles and is present with you, even when you feel distant from Him? In what ways does God's promise to be near the brokenhearted encourage you to reach out to Him? How could embracing this truth transform the way you respond to feelings of discouragement or isolation? Consider how understanding God's closeness could impact your journey through difficult seasons.

Real-World Example: Imagine someone who has recently lost a loved one—a parent, sibling, or close friend. In the days following the loss, they feel an overwhelming sense of emptiness and sorrow, struggling to make sense of a world without this cherished person. Every corner of their daily life brings reminders of the absence, deepening the feeling of being crushed in spirit. Yet, in the midst of their grief, friends and family members begin to gather around them. Some offer a quiet presence, sitting beside them in silence; others bring comforting words, memories, or small acts of kindness. Through these gestures, they begin to sense a glimmer of hope and peace, knowing they are not alone in their pain. These connections reflect the truth of Psalm 34:18—that even in their deepest sorrow, there is closeness and comfort, both from the people around them and from God, who draws near to the brokenhearted. This support doesn't erase the loss, but it becomes a foundation of strength, helping them face each day with a renewed sense of connection and resilience.

Small Prayer: Lord, thank You for being close to me when I am brokenhearted. Help me to feel Your presence and find reassurance in Your saving grace. Amen.

Wednesday: Overcoming Fear and Dismay

Explanation of the Topic: Isaiah 41:10 reminds us not to fear because God is with us. His promise to strengthen, help, and uphold us with His righteous right hand gives us the courage to face our fears and dismay, knowing that we are not alone.

Discussion Question: Isaiah 41:10 says, "Fear not, for I am with you; be not dismayed, for I am your God. I will strengthen you, I will help you, I will uphold you with my righteous right hand." Reflecting on this verse, think about the specific fears or moments of dismay you face in your life. How does knowing that God promises His presence and support influence your mindset? How does it help to know that God doesn't just observe your struggles but actively offers strength, help, and stability? Consider times when you've felt overwhelmed, alone, or anxious. How could reminding yourself of God's words here—especially His promise to uphold you with His "righteous right hand"—transform those moments? Think of it like having a reliable source of strength beside you. How might viewing God as an unwavering presence reduce your sense of fear, encourage you to move forward despite challenges, and remind you that you are never alone? As you explore this question, think about how you might begin to trust God more in specific areas of your life where fear or dismay has a strong hold.

Real-World Example: Imagine someone, Emma, who has recently received a life-altering health diagnosis. The news feels overwhelming, and a wave of fear and uncertainty washes over her as she tries to comprehend what this will mean for her future. She wrestles with thoughts of the challenges ahead—the treatments, the lifestyle changes, and the impact on her loved ones. Emma feels a deep sense of dismay and anxiety about her ability to endure what lies ahead. In her search for support, Emma joins a local support group where others share similar experiences. She meets people who have faced the same diagnosis, some who are still fighting and others who have come out on the other side. Listening to their stories, Emma feels both understood and encouraged. The group members share words of strength, wisdom, and faith, helping Emma realize she is not facing this journey alone. Through the words and presence of those who truly understand, Emma begins to feel a glimmer of hope. These supportive relationships become tangible reminders of God's promise in Isaiah 41:10. She reflects on the verse, finding comfort in knowing that God not only understands her fear but actively promises to strengthen and uphold her. With this support and a renewed faith, Emma finds courage to face each day, knowing that both God and her support community are there to help her navigate the path ahead. This experience teaches her that even in her moments of deepest fear and dismay, she can find strength and reassurance in the presence of God and the support of others who have been there before.

Small Prayer: God, when I am afraid and dismayed, remind me of Your presence and support. Strengthen me and help me to rely on Your righteous right hand. Amen.

Thursday: Finding Rest and Comfort in Jesus

Explanation of the Topic: Matthew 11:28-30 invites those who are weary and burdened to find rest in Jesus. His gentle and humble heart provides a place of comfort and peace. By coming to Him, we find relief from our burdens and rest for our souls.

Discussion Question: In Matthew 11:28-30, Jesus says, "Come to me, all you who are weary and burdened, and I will give you rest. Take my yoke upon you and learn from me, for I am gentle and humble in heart, and you will find rest for your souls. For my yoke is easy and my burden is light." Take a moment to reflect on the invitation Jesus offers here. What does it mean to truly come to Jesus when you're feeling exhausted, overwhelmed, or weighed down by life's challenges? How does it feel to know that Jesus offers a gentle, humble presence and invites you to find rest in Him? Think about times in your life when you've felt burdened by stress, expectations, or even spiritual struggles. What might it look like to release these burdens into Jesus' hands, trusting Him to carry what you cannot? Consider what "taking on His yoke" means—it's not a promise of a life free from hardship, but an invitation to share your struggles with someone who can carry them with you. How does knowing that Jesus' yoke is easy and His burden light change the way you approach difficult situations? Reflect on how Jesus' promise of rest could influence your daily life and your spiritual journey. How might it change the way you deal with stress or worry, knowing that you can find true comfort and rest in Him? Lastly, think about the kind of relationship Jesus is inviting you into: one that's built on trust, gentleness, and a shared journey. How can you respond to this invitation in practical ways, allowing His presence to bring you peace and strength?

Real-World Example: Imagine Maria, a busy parent juggling a demanding job, family responsibilities, and countless other daily tasks. Her days are filled with meetings, deadlines, and the needs of her children, often leaving her with little time to care for herself. She constantly feels as if she's running on empty, barely able to catch her breath before the next task or responsibility requires her attention. The weight of it all starts to feel overwhelming, and Maria finds herself exhausted, both physically and emotionally. One evening, after a particularly challenging day, Maria realizes that she needs to make a change to prevent burnout. She decides to carve out a small window of time each morning for quiet prayer and worship. Though it initially feels difficult to prioritize this time amidst her responsibilities, Maria begins each day by surrendering her worries to God, expressing her gratitude, and seeking strength for the day ahead. Over time, this practice becomes her lifeline. In those quiet moments, Maria feels a sense of peace washing over her, a kind of rest that goes beyond physical relaxation. She learns to release her anxieties and burdens to God, trusting Him to guide her through each day. This time of prayer and worship becomes a sacred space, allowing her to refocus her mind and find renewal. Through this experience, Maria comes to understand the truth of Matthew 11:28-30—that Jesus' invitation to "come to me, all you who are weary and burdened" is a real, accessible offer of peace and restoration. She learns that rest isn't just about having fewer tasks; it's about allowing God to carry the weight of her burdens and finding strength in His presence. This daily practice transforms her outlook, giving her a steady source of peace that sustains her through her hectic schedule.

Small Prayer: Jesus, I come to You with my weariness and burdens. Please give me rest and comfort, and help me to learn from Your gentle and humble heart. Amen.

Friday: Comforting Others

Explanation of the Topic: 2 Corinthians 1:3-4 teaches us that God is the source of all comfort, and He comforts us in our troubles so that we can comfort others. By sharing the comfort we receive from God, we can support and uplift those around us who are in despair.

Discussion Question: In 2 Corinthians 1:3-4, Paul writes, "Praise be to the God and Father of our Lord Jesus Christ, the Father of compassion and the God of all comfort, who comforts us in all our troubles, so that we can comfort those in any trouble with the comfort we ourselves receive from God." Reflect on what this passage reveals about the nature of God and His role as a source of comfort in our lives. How does experiencing

God's compassion and comfort in our own times of struggle prepare us to support others? Think about a time when you felt despair or deep sorrow and turned to God for strength. How did God's comfort sustain you? In what ways did that experience equip you to empathize with others who face similar struggles? Consider how sharing your own story of God's faithfulness could offer hope to someone going through their own season of despair. How might expressing your own vulnerability and compassion show others that they are not alone and that God's comfort is available to them as well? Additionally, what practical steps could you take to offer this comfort to others? Perhaps it involves actively listening, praying for them, or simply being present as a supportive friend. How can being a channel of God's compassion and comfort deepen your own faith as you witness God's work in someone else's life? Reflect on the impact that a genuine act of support can have in someone's journey through despair and how your actions might help them experience God's presence in a real and meaningful way.

Real-World Example: Imagine Michael, a man who went through a long and painful journey of recovery after a life-changing accident. The physical and emotional toll was overwhelming, and there were days when he questioned whether he would ever feel whole again. During this time, Michael found himself leaning heavily on his faith, seeking comfort in God's presence and relying on the support of friends and family. Over time, he discovered that God's compassion was sustaining him, providing peace even on his hardest days. The experience reshaped his faith, deepening his reliance on God and teaching him about resilience, hope, and healing. Years later, Michael meets others who are facing similar traumatic events—people struggling with the shock of sudden illness, unexpected loss, or debilitating injuries. Because he has been through this journey himself, he is able to offer support that goes beyond mere words. Michael can genuinely understand their fears, frustrations, and doubts, having faced them himself. He shares his story, not to dwell on his own pain, but to show others that healing is possible and that God's comfort is real. Michael organizes a small support group where people who have experienced life-altering challenges can come together to share their struggles and encourage one another. Through his guidance, group members begin to feel a sense of community and understanding. They find it easier to open up about their own pain and feel validated in their feelings. Michael reminds each person that God's comfort and peace are available to them just as they were to him, creating a safe space where they can encounter God's compassion.

This real-world example demonstrates how 2 Corinthians 1:3-4 comes alive in Michael's life. Through his own suffering and the comfort he received from God, he is equipped to comfort others. He has become a source of hope and reassurance, showing others that they are not alone and that God's love is a constant source of strength, even in life's darkest moments. His experience enables him to empathize deeply, to listen without judgment, and to gently point others toward God, fostering a supportive community that reminds each person of God's presence.

Small Prayer: Father of compassion, thank You for comforting me in my troubles. Help me to share Your comfort with others and be a source of support and encouragement. Amen.

End of the Week Closing Prayer for Spiritual Despair

"Dear Heavenly Father,

As this week comes to a close, I come before You with a heart that has faced both challenges and growth. Thank You for walking with me as I confronted my moments of despair and learned to find hope in You. When I acknowledged my feelings of heaviness, You reminded me that I am not alone—that You are near to the brokenhearted and ready to lift my burdens.

Lord, I am grateful for the reassurance of Your constant presence. Even in my darkest moments, I know that You are by my side, holding me up and providing strength. When fear and dismay seemed overwhelming, You reminded me of Your promise in Isaiah, that I do not need to be afraid because You are with me. Your strength sustains me and fills me with courage.

Thank You, Jesus, for inviting me to find rest in you. As I brought my burdens and weariness to You this week, You offered me a gentle, humble presence and a peace that goes beyond my understanding. Help me to remember that I can always come to You, even when life feels overwhelming, and that You will give me true rest.

And Lord, as I reflect on Your comfort and compassion, teach me to extend that same comfort to others. Help me to be a source of strength and encouragement to those who may be going through their own seasons of despair. May my journey with You be a testimony of Your love, so that I can share Your hope and peace with others who need it.

Thank You for this week of growth, reflection, and renewal. Guide me forward with a heart anchored in hope, resting in Your presence, and ready to comfort others with the compassion You have shown me.

In Jesus' name, Amen."

Week 2: Spiritual Emptiness

Introduction:

Spiritual emptiness is a profound sense of lacking meaning, purpose, or fulfillment in life. This condition can leave one feeling directionless and unfulfilled. The Bible provides wisdom and encouragement to help believers find true purpose and fulfillment in God.

Definition:

Spiritual Emptiness: A sense of lacking meaning, purpose, or fulfillment in life.

Key Scriptures:

Ecclesiastes 1:2 (NIV) - "'Meaningless! Meaningless!' says the Teacher. 'Utterly meaningless! Everything is meaningless.'"

Jeremiah 29:11 (NIV) - "'For I know the plans I have for you,' declares the Lord, 'plans to prosper you and not to harm you, plans to give you hope and a future.'"

John 10:10 (NIV) - "'The thief comes only to steal and kill and destroy; I have come that they may have life and have it to the full.'"

Romans 8:28 (NIV) - "'And we know that in all things God works for the good of those who love him, who have been called according to his purpose.'"

Philippians 4:13 (NIV) - "'I can do all this through him who gives me strength.'"

Monday: Recognizing Spiritual Emptiness

Explanation of Topic: Spiritual emptiness can manifest in feelings of dissatisfaction, lack of purpose, and a sense of something missing in our lives. Recognizing these signs is the first step towards seeking spiritual fulfillment.

Discussion Question: Based on the discussion and examples we've covered, make a detailed list of ways to identify signs of spiritual emptiness in your life. Reflect on both emotional and behavioral indicators, as well as changes in your relationship with God and others. Consider starting with emotional signs. For instance, do you feel a persistent sense of dissatisfaction, lack of purpose, or a void that you can't seem to fill, no matter what you do? Does your spiritual life feel flat or uninspired, as though something crucial is missing? Also, think about moments when you feel distant or disconnected from God. Are you finding it hard to find joy or meaning in activities that once strengthened your faith? Next, examine behavioral signs. Have you noticed a decrease in prayer, worship, or Bible reading, as though spiritual practices have lost their impact? Are you trying to fill this void with external distractions, such as excessive social media, entertainment, or even achievements, hoping these will give you the fulfillment you're missing? Lastly, look at your relationships and the way you interact with others. Do you feel isolated or as though connections with family, friends, or your faith community have weakened? Have you pulled back from relationships that used to uplift you spiritually? Reflect on how these signs might be indicating spiritual emptiness and consider how each of them can point you back to seeking fulfillment in God. As you identify these signs, think about practical steps you could take to address them and renew your sense of purpose and connection with God.

Real-World Example: Sarah is a dedicated mother juggling the many responsibilities of raising her children, managing her household, and staying active in her church community. She participates in Bible studies, volunteers regularly, and helps organize events at her church. From the outside, she appears fully engaged and spiritually active. Yet, despite all of this, Sarah feels an unshakable sense of emptiness and lack of fulfillment deep within her. Over time, Sarah begins to realize that this emptiness stems from a shift in her focus. She has become so immersed in fulfilling her duties and commitments that her personal connection with God has taken a back seat. She's been treating her spiritual life like another task on her checklist rather than nurturing it as a relationship. While she's physically present in her church activities, her heart feels distant, and she no longer experiences the joy and peace she once felt in her faith. One day, during a quiet moment, Sarah reflects on how busy her life has become and asks herself some difficult questions: Am I doing these activities out of a genuine desire to grow closer to God, or am I simply going through the motions? She realizes that while she's been involved in religious activities, she has not been prioritizing personal prayer, quiet reflection, or time spent alone with God. Her focus has been on doing rather than being with God. Acknowledging this, Sarah decides to make a change. She starts setting aside intentional time each day for personal prayer, Scripture meditation, and simply sitting in God's presence without any agenda. Gradually, she begins to feel her spiritual emptiness lifting. By prioritizing her relationship with God over her religious duties, Sarah rediscovers a sense of peace, purpose, and fulfillment that she had been missing. Her life is still busy, but now she approaches her responsibilities with renewed joy, knowing that her strength and fulfillment come from her personal connection with God, not just her involvement in church activities. This example highlights how easy it can be to mistake religious activity for spiritual health and how important it is to nurture a personal relationship with God beyond simply "doing" for Him.

Small Prayer: Lord, help me to recognize the signs of spiritual emptiness in my life and guide me towards finding true fulfillment in You. Amen.

Tuesday: Seeking God's Presence

Explanation of Topic: Actively seeking God's presence through prayer, worship, and Bible study can fill the void of spiritual emptiness and bring a sense of purpose and peace.

Discussion Question: How can actively seeking God's presence help us overcome feelings of spiritual emptiness? Think about the difference between knowing about God and truly experiencing Him in a personal way. Reflect on times when you have felt a void in your spiritual life. How did it feel to be spiritually "busy" but still unfulfilled? What changes when you intentionally seek God's presence, not just through activities, but by genuinely opening your heart to Him? Consider how seeking God's presence might impact your day-to-day experiences. When we're intentional about connecting with God, it's not just about ticking off tasks—it's about inviting Him into our thoughts, emotions, and daily moments. In what ways could setting aside quiet time with God, free from distractions, help you feel more fulfilled? How might practicing gratitude or simply sitting in silence before God help you sense His nearness and deepen your connection? Think, too, about how seeking God's presence reshapes our priorities. When we draw near to God, we often find that our perspectives change; worries can feel lighter, and we become more aware of His love and guidance. Reflect on how consistently seeking God's presence can renew your sense of purpose and align your heart with His. How might this shift from spiritual emptiness to spiritual fulfillment affect your relationships, decisions, and how you respond to challenges? Finally, consider practical ways to seek God's presence each day. This might include prayer, meditating on His Word, practicing worship, or even finding God in nature. How can these practices create space in your life for a deeper, more meaningful relationship with God that fills the emptiness?

Real-World Example: Tom is a successful businessman, known for his drive and achievements. His career has flourished—he has a well-paying job, a nice home, and the respect of his colleagues. Yet, despite these accomplishments, Tom feels a gnawing emptiness inside. He often finds himself wondering if there's more to life than the next big project or milestone. Even though he's reached many of his personal and professional goals, there's an unfulfilled part of him that he can't seem to ignore. One day, after a conversation with a friend, Tom decides to try something different. He begins setting aside time each morning to be alone with God. Rather than immediately diving into emails or planning his day, he starts each morning quietly, reading a passage from the Bible, reflecting on its message, and praying. This isn't easy at first; his mind often drifts to work tasks, and he's tempted to cut his quiet time short. But Tom persists, determined to cultivate a deeper relationship with God. As the days turn into weeks, Tom begins to notice subtle but powerful changes. The empty feeling he once carried starts to diminish, replaced by a quiet sense of peace he hadn't experienced before. His time with God each morning becomes something he looks forward to—a sacred moment that fills him up in a way his professional achievements never could. Through prayer and reflection, he feels a closeness to God that he hadn't thought was possible. This daily connection brings a new depth to his life, giving him a sense of purpose that goes beyond his career. In this newfound presence, Tom realizes that his fulfillment isn't tied to what he accomplishes but to who he is in God's eyes. He begins to approach his work with a fresh perspective, viewing his success as an opportunity to serve others rather than just a means to his own advancement. Tom's relationships with his family and friends also improve, as he's now able to give more of himself to them with a heart that feels whole and nourished. This experience teaches Tom that true fulfillment isn't something he can achieve through status or accomplishments alone. By seeking God's presence and prioritizing his relationship with Him, Tom discovers a lasting peace and contentment. His story shows that no matter how successful or busy we are, we all need to intentionally seek God's presence to find genuine purpose and satisfaction in our lives.

Small Prayer: Heavenly Father, draw me closer to You. Fill my heart with Your presence and let me find my fulfillment in You alone. Amen.

Wednesday: Filling the Void with God's Word

Explanation of Topic: God's Word is a source of comfort, guidance, and truth. Immersing ourselves in Scripture can fill our spiritual emptiness with God's promises and wisdom.

Discussion Question: Reflect on how God's Word can fill the emptiness we sometimes feel. In what ways does Scripture provide comfort, guidance, and a sense of purpose that external things—like possessions or social approval—cannot? Think about how verses of comfort, like Psalm 23, bring peace when you feel alone, and how verses like Jeremiah 29:11 give direction and hope, assuring us that God has a plan for us. Consider, too, how God's Word affirms our identity in Christ, reminding us that we're loved and valued, which fills us in ways the world cannot. How does understanding who you are in God's eyes address feelings of inadequacy? Lastly, think about how Scripture encourages gratitude and contentment, helping us focus on God's blessings rather than what we lack. Reflect on how comfort, purpose, identity, and gratitude in God's Word offer fulfillment that lasts. How can you make engaging with Scripture a habit to nurture your soul consistently?

Real World Example: After moving to a new city, Emma feels overwhelmed by loneliness. She misses the comfort of familiar faces and feels isolated in the unfamiliar environment. Hoping to find support, she joins a local Bible study group and begins to immerse herself in Scripture. As Emma reads verses about God's presence and faithfulness, such as Isaiah 41:10—"Do not fear, for I am with you"—she begins to experience a deep sense of peace and assurance. These words bring her comfort, reminding her that God is with her in every moment. The group becomes a supportive community, sharing their own stories of God's love, which encourages her to draw closer to Him. With time, the truths she finds in Scripture fill the void she once felt. Her relationship with God deepens, transforming her loneliness into a journey of spiritual growth and connection. Emma realizes that, even in a new city, she is never truly alone.

Small Prayer: Lord, let Your Word fill my heart and mind, replacing emptiness with Your truth and promises. Amen.

Thursday: Finding Fulfillment in Service

Explanation of Topic: Serving others shifts our focus from ourselves to those in need, allowing us to experience God's love in action and find fulfillment in making a difference.

Discussion Question: Reflect on how serving others can help to fill the emptiness you may feel in your own life. Think about the times when you've reached out to help someone—whether it was comforting a friend, volunteering at a shelter, or simply listening to someone who needed support. How does focusing on others' needs rather than your own shift your perspective? How does it impact the way you see your own challenges or feelings of emptiness? Consider, too, the inner joy and sense of purpose that often comes from serving. When you genuinely help someone, what do you feel deep down? Do you experience a sense of connection, fulfillment, or gratitude that wasn't there before? Reflect on how these feelings might come from knowing you're making a difference in someone else's life, even in small ways. Serving others allows you to experience a part of God's love, as you reflect His compassion and kindness to others.

Also, think about how serving others can draw you closer to God, helping you see life from His perspective. How might helping others strengthen your faith and remind you that your life has meaning beyond your personal struggles? Consider ways to make serving others a regular part of your life, allowing it to bring lasting purpose and peace into your heart.

Real World Example: After retiring from a 40-year career, James suddenly finds himself with a lot of free time and an unexpected sense of emptiness. For years, his job gave him a clear purpose, structure, and daily responsibilities, but now he feels a void where his sense of purpose used to be. He struggles with questions about his identity and worth, wondering what role he has left to play and how he can find meaning in this new stage of life. Seeking direction, James decides to start volunteering at a local shelter, initially just to stay busy. He begins by helping with simple tasks like serving meals, organizing supplies, and chatting with the shelter's visitors. Over time, though, James realizes that his role at the shelter is about more than just passing the time— it's about building connections and making a difference in the lives of others. He learns the names and stories of those who come to the shelter, and he starts looking forward to each day he spends there. Through this experience, James discovers a profound sense of joy and fulfillment that he hadn't anticipated. He finds that by shifting his focus away from himself and onto serving others, he feels more purposeful and alive. The gratitude and resilience he sees in those he serves inspire him, and he begins to sense a deeper connection to God. He feels as if God is working through him, using his time and compassion to impact others positively. This experience renews James's faith, giving him a sense of purpose he didn't realize was possible in retirement. Serving others not only fills the emptiness he once felt but also reconnects him to his community and his faith, showing him that his life still has significant purpose and value. Through his service, James finds peace, purpose, and a renewed sense of identity as a reflection of God's love in the world.

Small Prayer: Heavenly Father, help me to find fulfillment in serving others. Use my actions to reflect Your love and fill my heart with purpose. Amen

Friday: Building a Supportive Faith Community

Explanation of Topic: A supportive faith community provides encouragement, accountability, and shared experiences that can help us overcome spiritual emptiness and grow in our faith.

Discussion Question: Why is being part of a supportive faith community important in overcoming spiritual emptiness? Think about how a faith community provides encouragement, accountability, and shared experiences. When you're feeling empty or disconnected, having people who genuinely care about you can remind you that you're not alone and that others understand your struggles. A supportive community can also help you see God's work in action through others' stories, inspiring hope and strengthening your faith. How does hearing about others' experiences with God bring comfort and insight into your own challenges? Additionally, in times when it's hard to pray or feel close to God, a community can pray with you and for you, helping you carry burdens that feel too heavy on your own.

Reflect on how being part of such a community can fill your spirit, providing meaningful connections and reminding you of God's love through the support and fellowship of others.

Real World Example: Maria feels a deep sense of isolation and spiritual emptiness after moving to a new town. Without her usual support system, she finds it difficult to connect with others or feel grounded in her faith. After some hesitation, she decides to join a small group at her new church, hoping it might help ease her loneliness .As she starts attending, Maria is welcomed warmly and finds herself surrounded by people who genuinely care about her well-being. In this group, she finds more than just casual friendships; she discovers a supportive community that shares her faith and values. Group members encourage her, pray for her, and share their own struggles, reminding her that she's not alone in her spiritual journey. Over time, Maria feels a renewed sense of spiritual connection and fulfillment. Through shared worship, meaningful discussions, and the comfort of genuine companionship, she realizes that her faith is deepening, and her sense of belonging is growing. This community becomes a source of strength, helping her feel grounded and spiritually whole once again.

Small Prayer: Lord, thank You for the gift of community. Help me to connect with others who will encourage and support me in my spiritual journey. Amen.

End of the Week Closing Prayer for Spiritual Emptiness

"Dear Heavenly Father,

Thank You for guiding me through this week as I've confronted the emptiness within. You know every part of my heart, and I thank You for showing me that only You can truly fill the void I sometimes feel. Lord, help me to recognize when my spirit feels empty and to turn to You, rather than the temporary things of this world.

Teach me to fill my heart and mind with Your Word, that I may be rooted in Your truth and strengthened by Your promises. When I feel a sense of lack, remind me that Your Word is a wellspring of life, hope, and purpose. May Your words fill me up, renew my spirit, and guide my steps each day.

Help me find fulfillment by serving others, Lord, knowing that You created us to love and care for one another. Show me opportunities to extend a helping hand, to offer kindness, and to share the love You've given me. Through service, may I experience the joy and purpose that come from reflecting Your heart.

Thank You for the gift of community, Lord. Surround me with people who encourage me, challenge me, and walk with me in faith. Help me build a network of friends and mentors who will support me in my journey and draw me closer to You. When I feel isolated, remind me of the strength and comfort found in a faith community.

Most of all, Lord, teach me to seek Your presence above all else. When I'm feeling lost, empty, or unfulfilled, help me remember that You are near and that Your love is more than enough. May I always turn to You, seeking the peace, joy, and purpose that only You can provide.

Thank You for filling my emptiness with Your love and guiding me to find my true fulfillment in You. Draw me closer to Your heart, Lord, and help me live each day in the light of Your grace.

In Jesus' name, Amen."

Week 3: Spiritual Isolation

Introduction:

Spiritual isolation is a profound sense of feeling disconnected from others and from God. This condition can lead to loneliness and a sense of abandonment. However, the Bible provides insight, comfort, and guidance on overcoming spiritual isolation and restoring a sense of connection with God and others.

Definition:

Spiritual isolation: refers to a state in which an individual experiences a profound sense of disconnection, either from their faith, from other people, or from a higher power. This feeling of separation can occur even when a person is physically present in religious or social environments, indicating that the disconnection is more profound than just physical isolation. It often involves feelings of abandonment, loneliness, and alienation in relation to one's spiritual beliefs or the divine presence.

Key Scriptures:

Psalm 27:10 (NIV) - "Though my father and mother forsake me, the Lord will receive me."

Hebrews 10:24-25 (NIV) - " "And let us consider how we may spur one another on toward love and good deeds, not giving up meeting together, as some are in the habit of doing, but encouraging one another—and all the more as you see the Day approaching."

Romans 8:38-39 (NIV) - " "For I am convinced that neither death nor life, neither angels nor demons, neither the present nor the future, nor any powers, neither height nor depth, nor anything else in all creation, will be able to separate us from the love of God that is in Christ Jesus our Lord."

John 15:5 (NIV) "I am the vine; you are the branches. If you remain in me and I in you, you will bear much fruit; apart from me you can do nothing."

1 Corinthians 12:12-14 (NIV) - Just as a body, though one, has many parts, but all its many parts form one body, so it is with Christ. For we were all baptized by one Spirit so as to form one body—whether Jews or Gentiles, slave or free—and we were all given the one Spirit to drink. Even so the body is not made up of one part but of many."

Monday: Feeling Abandoned by Friends and Family

Explanation of Topic: Feeling abandoned can lead to spiritual isolation, making us doubt our value and relationship with God. The Bible reminds us that God is always with us, even when others are not.

Discussion Question: How does feeling abandoned by those closest to you impact your day-to-day life and your spiritual journey? Consider how such feelings can create a deep sense of loneliness, perhaps leading you to question your self-worth or even your purpose. Does it cause you to withdraw emotionally, struggle with trust, or feel hesitant to open up to others? Reflect on how this affects your view of yourself and your relationships. In terms of your spiritual journey, feeling abandoned can lead to doubts about God's presence or love, especially if you feel He's distant during tough times. It might make prayer or worship feel difficult or empty, as though God is just as far away as the people you've lost. If you could put these feelings into words, what would they be? Would it sound like "I feel unseen," "I'm not worthy of love," or "God, where are You in this?" Expressing these emotions can help bring clarity, revealing the areas where you need healing and support.

Real-World Example: Sarah, a young woman, recently relocated to a new city with hopes of fresh opportunities and meaningful friendships. Despite her best efforts to stay connected with her old friends, calling, texting, and sharing updates—she feels increasingly distant. Her friends seem to have moved on without her, seldom reaching out or including her in their lives. As weeks pass, Sarah's feelings of isolation deepen, and she begins to question her own value and significance. She wrestles with a sense of abandonment, wondering if her friendships were ever as genuine as she thought, and she starts doubting her self-worth and purpose in this new chapter of life.

Small Prayer: Lord, help me to feel Your presence when I feel abandoned by others. Remind me that You are always with me and that I am never truly alone. Amen.

Tuesday: Struggling to Find a Church Community

Explanation of Topic: Finding a supportive church community is crucial for spiritual growth and connection. It provides a sense of belonging and encouragement in our faith journey.

Discussion Question: How important is a church community in overcoming spiritual isolation? Reflect on how being part of a church community can provide meaningful connections, support, and encouragement. When facing spiritual isolation, having people who share your beliefs and values can offer companionship and understanding that help you feel seen and supported. A church community also creates opportunities for shared worship, prayer, and learning, which can draw you closer to God and remind you that you're part of a larger family of faith. How does being around others who openly live out their faith inspire you in your own spiritual journey? Consider, too, how participating in church activities, like small groups or volunteer opportunities, can help break down feelings of isolation by fostering a sense of belonging and purpose. Reflect on how a supportive church community might not only alleviate feelings of loneliness but also strengthen your relationship with God as you experience His love through others.

Real-World Example: John recently moved to a new town, leaving behind a strong faith community that had been a vital part of his life. In his new environment, he struggles to find a church where he feels welcomed and connected. Week after week, he visits different congregations, but he hasn't yet found one that feels like home. Without the familiar support and shared worship he once enjoyed, John begins to feel spiritually isolated and adrift. His faith feels distant, and he misses the encouragement and accountability that came from being part of a close-knit church community. This lack of connection leaves him feeling not only alone but also spiritually disconnected, as he longs to find a place where he can rebuild a sense of belonging and spiritual grounding.

Small Prayer: Lord, guide me to a church community where I can grow in faith and find support. Help me to build meaningful relationships that draw me closer to You. Amen.

Wednesday: Overwhelmed by Life's Challenges

Explanation of Topic: Life's challenges can consume our time and energy, making it hard to maintain our spiritual practices. Prioritizing our relationship with God helps us stay connected and find strength in Him.

Discussion Question: How can life's challenges contribute to feelings of spiritual isolation? Think about how difficult circumstances—such as illness, loss, financial struggles, or relationship conflicts—can make you feel distant from God and others. In these moments, it's easy to feel like no one truly understands what you're going through, leading you to withdraw emotionally and spiritually. Reflect on how these challenges might cause you to question God's presence or purpose, sometimes leaving you feeling abandoned or overlooked. Does it make prayer or worship harder, as if God is distant or unresponsive? Consider how feelings of isolation can build up, especially if you're carrying your burdens alone without sharing them with trusted friends or a faith community. Think about ways to reconnect spiritually and find support, even when challenges seem overwhelming. Reaching out to others or spending time in Scripture might remind you that you're not alone in your struggles, and that God is present even in life's toughest moments.

Real-World Example: Maria is juggling a demanding job, family responsibilities, and mounting financial stress. Each day feels like a race to get everything done, leaving her emotionally and physically drained. As her workload grows, she finds it harder to carve out time for prayer or Bible study, the practices that once grounded her. The pressures of daily life keep pulling her away from her spiritual habits, and gradually, Maria starts to feel a deep sense of spiritual isolation. She misses the peace she used to find in her faith but feels stuck in a cycle of exhaustion, unable to reconnect with God. The distance grows, and she begins to question if God is aware of her struggles or if He's listening at all. The weight of her responsibilities and lack of spiritual renewal leave Maria feeling more alone than ever, longing for the closeness with God that once sustained her.

Small Prayer: Heavenly Father, help me to prioritize my relationship with You amidst life's challenges. Give me the strength and wisdom to manage my responsibilities while staying close to You. Amen.

Thursday: Experiencing Doubt and Uncertainty

Explanation of Topic: Doubt can lead to spiritual isolation by creating a sense of separation from God. Addressing our doubts through prayer, study, and seeking counsel can help restore our connection with God.

Discussion Question: How does doubt affect your sense of spiritual connection? Reflect on how feelings of doubt—whether about God's presence, His love, or His plans—can create a barrier between you and Him. When doubt creeps in, it often leads to questioning your faith, feeling uncertain in prayer, or wondering if God is really listening. This sense of uncertainty can make it harder to feel His presence or trust in His promises, leaving you feeling distant or disconnected spiritually.

Think about how doubt might cause you to pull back, becoming less engaged in worship, prayer, or reading Scripture. When you're struggling to believe fully, it's easy to feel as though you're on the outside, looking in. Reflect on how acknowledging these doubts and bringing them to God could actually strengthen your faith, reminding you that He meets you where you are, even in moments of uncertainty.

Real-World Example: Tom has been wrestling with deep-seated doubts about his faith, questioning whether God is truly present and active in his life. He feels uncertain during prayer, wondering if his words are even being heard, and finds himself struggling to engage with Scripture. The doubts he's experiencing have created an invisible wall, leaving him feeling isolated and disconnected from the faith that once grounded him. As he continues to grapple with these questions, Tom notices a sense of emptiness growing. He longs to feel close to God again, but his uncertainty makes him hesitant to fully trust or open his heart. The spiritual isolation he feels only reinforces his doubts, creating a cycle that's hard to break. Tom feels caught between a desire to believe and the weight of his questions, unsure of how to rebuild the connection he's lost.

Small Prayer: Lord, help me to overcome my doubts and uncertainties. Strengthen my faith and draw me closer to You. Remind me of Your presence and love in my life. Amen.

Friday: Navigating Personal Loss

Explanation of Topic: Personal loss can lead to deep feelings of grief and spiritual isolation. Turning to God for comfort and allowing ourselves to grieve can help us find healing and restore our connection with Him.

Discussion Question: How can personal loss lead to feelings of spiritual isolation? Think about how losing a loved one, a relationship, or even a job can bring a deep sense of grief and emptiness. These losses often cause us to question God's purpose, His goodness, or even His presence in our lives. In moments of intense pain, it can feel as if God is distant, leading to feelings of abandonment or isolation. Reflect on how grief might make it difficult to pray or find comfort in Scripture, as though God isn't as near as He once felt. Personal loss can also lead to withdrawing from friends or faith communities, creating a further sense of isolation. Consider how opening up about these struggles with trusted people or bringing them to God could be a first step in reconnecting spiritually, even amidst the

Real World Example: Emma recently lost a beloved family member, and the grief she feels is overwhelming. Every day, she struggles with the weight of sadness and a profound sense of emptiness that seems impossible to fill. The loss has shaken her deeply, and she finds it hard to go through her normal spiritual practices; prayer feels hollow, and reading Scripture doesn't bring the comfort it once did. Emma's sorrow makes her feel distant from God, as though He's far away in this season of pain. She longs to feel His presence and comfort but instead feels spiritually disconnected, unsure of how to approach Him in her grief. Her usual support systems don't seem to reach the depth of her pain, leaving her feeling isolated and alone in both her faith and her sorrow. Emma wonders if God truly understands the depth of her loss, which only adds to her sense of spiritual isolation.

Small Prayer: Lord, comfort me in my time of loss. Help me to feel Your presence and love as I navigate my grief. Draw me closer to You and provide the peace and healing that only You can give. Amen.

End of the Week Closing Prayer for Spiritual Isolation

"Dear Heavenly Father,

As I come to the end of this week, I bring before You the struggles and feelings of isolation that have weighed on my heart. Lord, I acknowledge the times I have felt abandoned by friends and family, wondering if I am alone in my journey. Help me to remember that You are always with me, even when others may not be, and that Your love is constant and unchanging.

In moments when life's challenges feel overwhelming and I don't know where to turn, give me the strength to seek Your guidance and peace. Help me to find comfort in knowing that You understand every burden I carry and that I am never without Your support.

Lord, I also lift up my desire to find a church community where I feel truly connected. Lead me to people who will encourage and uplift me in my walk with You, who will walk beside me in both joy and sorrow. May I remember that wherever I go, Your Spirit goes with me, connecting me to a larger family of faith.

When I am plagued by doubts and uncertainty, remind me that my questions do not distance me from You but are a natural part of growing closer to You. Help me to embrace my doubts as a way to deepen my understanding and trust in Your presence, even when I cannot see the way forward.

And in the sorrow of personal loss, when grief feels too heavy to bear, hold me close and be my source of comfort. Help me to feel Your loving presence surrounding me, filling the emptiness that loss can leave behind. Remind me that You are near to the brokenhearted and that I am not alone in my pain.

Thank You, Lord, for walking with me through this week. Help me to hold on to the hope that You are my constant companion, even in times of spiritual isolation. May I continue to seek Your presence and trust in Your love as I move forward, knowing that You are with me every step of the way.

In Jesus' name, Amen."

Week 4: Spiritual Guilt

Introduction

Spiritual guilt arises when we feel remorse or regret for actions that we believe have violated our faith or moral values. It can be a powerful tool for spiritual growth when it leads to genuine repentance and a closer relationship with God. However, it can also become a burden if not properly addressed and resolved through God's grace and forgiveness.

Definition

Spiritual Guilt: A feeling of remorse or regret for actions that violate one's faith or moral values, which can lead to either spiritual growth or a burdensome sense of condemnation.

Key Scriptures

1 John 1:9 (NIV)-"If we confess our sins, he is faithful and just and will forgive us our sins and purify us from all unrighteousness."

Psalm 32:5 (NIV)-"Then I acknowledged my sin to you and did not cover up my iniquity. I said, 'I will confess my transgressions to the Lord.' And you forgave the guilt of my sin."

Romans 8:1 (NIV)-"Therefore, there is now no condemnation for those who are in Christ Jesus."

Hebrews 10:22 (NIV)-"Let us draw near to God with a sincere heart and with the full assurance that faith brings, having our hearts sprinkled to cleanse us from a guilty conscience and having our bodies washed with pure water."

Psalm 103:12 (NIV)-"As far as the east is from the west, so far has he removed our transgressions from us."

Monday: The Weight of Guilt

Explanation of Topic: Guilt can be a heavy burden that affects our mental and emotional well-being, causing us to withdraw from relationships and from God.

Discussion Question: How does carrying the weight of guilt impact your relationship with God and others? Reflect on how guilt often creates a barrier, making us feel unworthy of love and forgiveness. When we carry unresolved guilt, we may distance ourselves from God, feeling too ashamed or afraid to approach Him. This can make prayer and worship feel empty, as though a part of us is holding back. Guilt can also strain our relationships with others, causing us to withdraw out of fear of judgment or rejection. It may prevent us from being honest or vulnerable, as we struggle with feelings of inadequacy. Consider how holding onto guilt can isolate us, limiting the love and support we're able to give and receive. How might releasing guilt and embracing forgiveness help you reconnect with both God and the people around you?

Real-World Example: Sarah told a lie to her close friend, a decision she quickly regretted. The guilt began to consume her thoughts, filling her with a sense of shame and self-blame. Each night, Sarah found herself replaying the lie in her mind, unable to sleep as she worried about the consequences and felt disappointed in herself. Instead of addressing the issue, she began to avoid her friend out of fear of confrontation or further disappointment. This guilt-driven avoidance created distance, not only isolating her from her friend but also causing her to feel increasingly alone and disconnected. The weight of unaddressed guilt prevented Sarah from finding peace or restoring trust in her relationship.

Small Prayer: Lord, help me to release the burden of guilt and seek Your forgiveness. Restore my relationships and draw me closer to You. Amen.

Tuesday: Confessing Our Sins

Explanation of Topic: Confessing our sins is crucial for spiritual healing. It allows us to experience God's forgiveness and begin the journey towards restoration

Discussion Question: How does confessing our sins to God bring relief and restoration? Reflect on how keeping our sins hidden can create a burden of guilt, leading to feelings of shame, isolation, and even distance from God. When we confess, we bring these hidden struggles into the light, allowing us to release the weight of guilt we've been carrying. Confessing to God reminds us that He is compassionate and ready to forgive, which can be deeply healing. It helps us reconnect with Him, knowing that He doesn't hold our past mistakes against us but offers grace and a fresh start. In what ways does opening up to God about our struggles lead to a sense of peace, freedom, and the chance to rebuild our relationship with Him and others?

Real-World Example: John had been struggling with a hidden addiction for months, and the guilt of keeping it a secret weighed heavily on him. He felt trapped, ashamed, and distant from both God and those who cared about him. Finally, overwhelmed by the burden, John decided to open up. He confessed his struggle to God, laying his guilt and pain before Him, and then shared his struggle with a trusted mentor. This moment of honesty was a powerful turning point. By bringing his struggle into the open, John felt an immediate sense of relief and a glimmer of hope he hadn't felt in a long time. His confession allowed him to experience God's forgiveness and created a pathway for healing. With his mentor's support, John now had someone to hold him accountable and encourage him on his journey toward recovery, helping him rebuild his faith and regain control over his life.

Small Prayer: Heavenly Father, give me the courage to confess my sins to You. Thank You for Your promise of forgiveness and purification. Amen.

Wednesday: Embracing God's Forgiveness

Explanation of Topic: Embracing God's forgiveness allows us to see our past through the lens of grace, enabling us to learn from our mistakes and grow spiritually.

Discussion Question: How can embracing God's forgiveness change your perspective on past mistakes? Reflect on how carrying regret and shame over past mistakes often distorts how we see ourselves, making us feel defined by those actions. When we fully accept God's forgiveness, however, we're reminded that our identity is rooted in His love and grace, not in our past errors. God's forgiveness allows us to see mistakes as opportunities for growth rather than permanent failures. Instead of feeling weighed down, we can move forward with a sense of renewal and purpose. How might this shift in perspective free you to forgive yourself, make amends, and build a healthier relationship with God and others? Embracing forgiveness helps us let go of the past and live more fully in the freedom that God offers.

Real-World Example: Maria had been carrying guilt over several past mistakes, feeling haunted by regret and unworthy of peace. This guilt affected her confidence, her relationships, and even her faith, as she struggled to forgive herself. One day, after a heartfelt prayer, she decided to fully embrace God's forgiveness, trusting that He had wiped her slate clean. This acceptance brought Maria a deep sense of relief and peace that she hadn't experienced in years. With her burdens lifted, she was able to see herself through God's eyes—as loved and redeemed, not defined by her past. As she moved forward, Maria found herself drawn to helping others who carried similar struggles, using her story to encourage them to find freedom in God's grace. Her journey from guilt to grace gave her purpose, helping her see how God could use her story to bring hope to others

Small Prayer: Lord, help me to truly accept Your forgiveness and let go of my past mistakes. Fill my heart with Your peace. Amen.

Thursday: Living Without Condemnation

Explanation of Topic: Living without condemnation means understanding that, in Christ, we are free from the guilt and shame of our past sins. We are made new and can live in the freedom of God's grace.

Discussion Question: What does it mean to live without condemnation, according to Romans 8:1? In this verse, Paul writes, "Therefore, there is now no condemnation for those who are in Christ Jesus." Living without condemnation means that, through Jesus, we are no longer judged or defined by our past sins and mistakes. God's grace frees us from the guilt and shame that once weighed us down, allowing us to walk in forgiveness and new life. Reflect on how this freedom changes the way we see ourselves and approach our relationship with God. Rather than living in fear or shame, we can live confidently, knowing we are accepted and loved. How does this shift from condemnation to grace encourage you to grow spiritually, and how might it influence the way you approach both God and others? Living without condemnation invites us to embrace the peace, joy, and purpose that come from knowing we are fully forgiven.

Real-World Example: David spent years feeling burdened by guilt over his past mistakes, convinced that he was unworthy of God's love. This sense of unworthiness held him back, affecting his self-image and his ability to connect with God. Then, one day, while studying Romans 8:1, he encountered the life-changing truth: "There is now no condemnation for those who are in Christ Jesus." Realizing that God didn't condemn him, David began to see himself differently—not as someone defined by past failures, but as someone fully loved and forgiven. Embracing this truth brought him a new sense of freedom and confidence. His relationship with God deepened as he felt able to approach Him without shame, and his renewed faith inspired him to live with purpose, knowing he was accepted in Christ. This shift transformed not only his self-image but also his daily walk with God, as he learned to see himself as God sees him.

Small Prayer: Jesus, thank You for freeing me from condemnation. Help me to live in the freedom and joy of Your grace every day. Amen.

Friday: The Power of a Clean Conscience

Explanation of Topic: A clean conscience allows us to live with peace and joy, positively affecting our relationships and our overall well-being. It is a testament to God's transformative power in our lives.

Discussion Question: How does having a clean conscience through Christ affect your daily life? When we accept Christ's forgiveness, we're freed from the guilt and shame that often weigh us down, giving us a clean conscience. This sense of freedom impacts how we approach each day, allowing us to live with peace and confidence, rather than fear or regret. With a clean conscience, we feel more open to connect with God in prayer and worship, no longer held back by feelings of unworthiness. It also affects our relationships with others, empowering us to be honest, compassionate, and more forgiving, as we're no longer burdened by past mistakes. Reflect on how this freedom in Christ allows you to embrace each day with a renewed sense of purpose and joy, knowing you are fully accepted and loved.

Real World Example:Emma had been carrying a heavy sense of guilt after speaking harshly to her sibling during an argument. The memory of her words lingered, affecting her peace of mind and straining their relationship. Over time, the guilt grew, making her feel distant from both her sibling and God. Finally, Emma decided to seek forgiveness. She approached God in prayer, confessing her actions, and then apologized sincerely to her sibling. After receiving forgiveness from both, Emma felt a profound sense of relief and a clean conscience. The weight of guilt lifted, bringing her a deep sense of joy and inner peace. This clean conscience not only renewed her relationship with her sibling but also strengthened her connection with God, allowing her to move forward without the shadow of past mistakes. The experience taught Emma the power of forgiveness and the freedom that comes from seeking reconciliation.

Small Prayer: Lord, cleanse my conscience from guilt. Let me live each day in the peace and joy that comes from being forgiven and loved by You. Amen.

End of the Week Closing Prayer for Spiritual Guilt

"Dear Lord,

As I close this week, I bring before You all that I've learned and experienced in dealing with the weight of guilt. Thank You for guiding me to see that I don't have to carry these burdens alone. When guilt tries to hold me back, You remind me of the power of living with a clean conscience, the freedom that comes from knowing that my sins are forgiven in You.

This week, You showed me the truth of living without condemnation. Through Jesus, I am free from the labels of my past mistakes, and I am accepted just as I am. Help me to live confidently in this freedom, knowing that my worth is not defined by what I've done but by who I am in You.

Thank You for the courage to confess my sins, Lord. In doing so, I found relief and peace, knowing that honesty with You brings closeness and healing. I am grateful for Your love that meets me exactly where I am, with open arms and a heart full of compassion.

I also thank You for the incredible gift of forgiveness. Help me to embrace it fully, to let go of any lingering shame, and to see myself through Your eyes—as loved, valued, and redeemed. When guilt tries to creep back into my heart, let me remember that Your forgiveness is greater and more powerful than any mistake I've made.

As I move forward, may I carry a renewed spirit, a clean conscience, and a heart that rests in Your grace. Let these lessons transform me, freeing me from the weight of guilt and filling me with the joy of knowing I am fully forgiven and loved.

In Jesus' name, Amen."

Week 5: Spiritual Pride

Introduction:

Spiritual pride is an excessive sense of one's spiritual superiority or enlightenment. It can hinder one's relationship with God and others, leading to judgmental attitudes and a lack of humility. The Bible warns against spiritual pride and teaches the importance of humility and recognizing our dependence on God.

Definition: Spiritual Pride: An excessive sense of one's spiritual superiority or enlightenment.

Key Scriptures:

Proverbs 16:18 (NIV) - "Pride goes before destruction, a haughty spirit before a fall."

Luke 18:9-14 (NIV) - The parable of the Pharisee and the tax collector.

James 4:6 (NIV) - "But he gives us more grace. That is why Scripture says: 'God opposes the proud but shows favor to the humble.'"

Philippians 2:3-4 (NIV) - "Do nothing out of selfish ambition or vain conceit. Rather, in humility value others above yourselves..."

1 Corinthians 4:7 (NIV) - "For who makes you different from anyone else? What do you have that you did not receive?"

Monday: Recognizing Spiritual Pride

Explanation of Topic: Spiritual pride can manifest subtly, making individuals feel superior to others due to their spiritual knowledge, status, or experiences. Recognizing these signs is the first step toward humility.

Discussion Question: How can you identify signs of spiritual pride in your own life? Reflect on moments when you may have felt a sense of superiority over others in your faith or judged others based on their beliefs or spiritual practices. Spiritual pride often appears subtly, such as when we become resistant to correction, assume we have all the answers, or take more credit for our growth than we attribute to God. Consider if there are times when you focus more on appearing "right" or "holy" rather than growing humbly in your relationship with God. Do you find it difficult to admit weaknesses or ask for help, feeling as though you should have everything figured out? Recognizing these tendencies is essential in surrendering pride and opening ourselves to God's transformative work. Reflecting on these signs can help you cultivate humility and a heart that seeks to learn and grow closer to God.

Real-World Example: A church leader named Mark has dedicated years to serving his congregation, gaining extensive knowledge of Scripture and experience in ministry. Over time, however, Mark begins to feel a subtle shift in his attitude. He starts seeing himself as more spiritually advanced than those he leads, believing his position and knowledge set him apart. This sense of superiority makes him less open to feedback from others, feeling that his insights are more valuable or correct simply because of his role. As members of his church or fellow leaders offer suggestions or constructive feedback, Mark finds himself dismissive or defensive, unwilling to consider that he might need growth or correction. His pride creates a distance between him and his congregation, limiting his ability to connect with others authentically. Eventually, this attitude affects his ministry, as people feel they cannot approach him openly, sensing his reluctance to receive guidance. Mark's journey shows how unchecked spiritual pride can impact relationships, hinder growth, and weaken one's connection to the community and God's ongoing work in their life.

Small Prayer: Lord, help me to recognize any prideful tendencies in my heart. Grant me the humility to see myself and others through Your eyes. Amen.

Tuesday: The Danger of Comparing Ourselves to Others

Explanation of Topic: Comparing ourselves to others can lead to pride if we feel superior or to discouragement if we feel inferior. God calls us to focus on our unique journey with Him.

Discussion Question: How can comparing yourself to others lead to spiritual pride? When we measure our spiritual growth, practices, or knowledge against others, it's easy to start feeling either superior or inferior. If we see ourselves as "doing better" in areas like prayer, Scripture knowledge, or church involvement, it can create a subtle sense of pride, making us feel more righteous or "closer to God" than others. This attitude shifts our focus away from God and onto our own achievements, leading us to judge others' journeys and become less receptive to our own need for growth. Comparing ourselves to others can make us blind to areas where we still need God's grace and transformation, limiting our humility and ability to connect genuinely with those around us. Reflect on how focusing on your own journey with God, rather than comparing, can help keep your heart centered on His love and grace.

Real-World Example: Lisa, a devoted Christian, finds herself frequently comparing her spiritual life to those around her. At church, she notices how often others volunteer, their deep knowledge of Scripture, or the way they express their faith openly. Sometimes, Lisa feels a sense of inadequacy, doubting her own commitment or feeling like she's not "spiritual enough." But at other times, she finds herself feeling superior, judging others who don't seem as involved or disciplined in their faith practices as she is. These comparisons start to shift Lisa's focus away from her personal relationship with God. Instead of nurturing her own spiritual growth, she becomes preoccupied with how she measures up to those around her. This cycle of comparison leads her to either strive for validation from others or quietly feel self-satisfied, thinking her practices make her more faithful. Eventually, Lisa realizes that these feelings are creating a barrier between her and God, as she's no longer seeking His approval but rather validation through comparison. Her journey highlights how spiritual pride or inadequacy can take root when we lose sight of our unique walk with God, and how focusing on others can prevent us from fully embracing His grace in our own lives.

Small Prayer: Heavenly Father, keep me from the trap of comparison. Help me to focus on my relationship with You and to celebrate the unique path You have for me. Amen.

Wednesday: The Role of Humility

Explanation of Topic: Humility acknowledges that all we have and achieve is by God's grace. It keeps us grounded and open to God's correction and leading.

Discussion Question: How does humility protect us from spiritual pride? Humility shifts our focus away from self-centered comparisons or achievements and keeps us grounded in our dependence on God's grace. By recognizing that all growth and understanding come from Him, we're less likely to feel superior to others or take credit for our spiritual journey. Humility reminds us that we're all works in progress and that we need God's ongoing guidance and forgiveness. With humility, we become more open to correction and learning, seeing our faith as a journey rather than a destination where we "arrive." This openness protects us from looking down on others and instead fosters a heart of compassion, knowing that we, too, have areas of weakness. Reflect on how humility keeps us connected to God's love, creating a genuine desire to serve Him and others rather than seeking validation or praise. In this way, humility acts as a safeguard, ensuring our faith remains rooted in grace rather than pride

Real World Example: James is a respected ministry leader with a thriving congregation and numerous successful outreach programs. Many look up to him for his dedication and leadership skills, but James is careful to attribute all of his accomplishments to God's grace. Rather than viewing his successes as personal achievements, he constantly reminds himself—and others—that his ministry's growth is a result of God's blessing and guidance. James regularly seeks God's direction in prayer, approaching each new challenge with a heart open to learning. He consults his mentors and remains receptive to feedback, understanding that his role is to serve rather than to be served. This humility helps James stay grounded, keeping him focused on God's mission rather than on building his own reputation. His approach not only protects him from spiritual pride but also sets an example for his congregation, showing them that true leadership comes from relying on God and maintaining a teachable spirit. Through his humility, James cultivates a ministry rooted in grace, service, and continual growth.

Small Prayer: Lord Jesus, You modeled perfect humility. Teach me to walk humbly with You, recognizing that all I am and have is because of Your grace. Amen.

Thursday: Serving Others Selflessly

Explanation of Topic: Serving others shifts our focus from ourselves to the needs of others. It fosters humility and reminds us that we are all equal in God's eyes, created to serve one another.

Discussion Question: How can serving others help combat spiritual pride? When we serve others, especially those in need, it shifts our focus away from ourselves and reminds us of our shared humanity and dependence on God's grace. Serving puts us in a position of humility, where we see that everyone has value and that we are all equal before God. Serving others also teaches us compassion, patience, and selflessness, qualities that help counteract pride. By prioritizing others' needs over our own, we're reminded that true spiritual growth comes from loving and uplifting those around us, not from status or recognition. Reflect on how serving allows you to see yourself as God's instrument, reinforcing that any abilities or blessings you have are meant to bless others and glorify Him, rather than elevate yourself. In this way, service becomes a powerful antidote to spiritual pride, fostering humility and a heart aligned with God's purposes.

Real World Example: Rachel is a devoted believer who volunteers consistently at her local food pantry and community center. Each week, she dedicates her time to packing meals, sorting donations, and connecting with people who come in for support. Rachel finds genuine joy in helping others, and her heart is focused on serving rather than being noticed or praised. She doesn't look for acknowledgment from others; instead, she feels fulfilled knowing that her efforts are making a difference in people's lives. Through her service, Rachel is reminded of the shared struggles and strengths of her community, which keeps her grounded and grateful. She sees her role as simply being an extension of God's love, understanding that her skills and resources are blessings meant to uplift others. By focusing on meeting others' needs, Rachel maintains a humble perspective, recognizing that her service is ultimately about honoring God rather than building her own reputation. This mindset protects her from spiritual pride, allowing her to serve with a heart full of compassion and humility.

Small Prayer: Father, grant me a servant's heart. Help me to serve others with love and humility, reflecting Christ's love in all I do. Amen.

Friday: Dependence on God

Explanation of Topic: Dependence on God acknowledges our limitations and His sovereignty. It keeps us humble, recognizing that our strength and wisdom come from Him alone

Discussion Question: Why is it important to maintain dependence on God to avoid spiritual pride? Dependence on God keeps us grounded, reminding us that all growth, wisdom, and strength come from Him, not from our own abilities. When we rely on God daily, we recognize our limitations and the need for His guidance, which fosters humility. This dependence prevents us from falling into the trap of self-sufficiency, where we might start to believe we're responsible for our own spiritual achievements. Acknowledging our need for God allows us to see ourselves as instruments in His hands, rather than as the source of success. It keeps us open to correction and learning, knowing that our journey with God requires His ongoing grace and support. Dependence on Him helps us avoid spiritual pride by keeping our focus on His greatness rather than on our own accomplishments, cultivating a spirit of humility and gratitude.

Real World Example: Michael is a committed believer who finds himself in a difficult season, facing challenges at work and within his family. Instead of relying solely on his own skills or knowledge to fix these issues, he turns to God each day in prayer, humbly asking for wisdom and strength. Michael acknowledges his limitations, understanding that without God's guidance, his efforts may fall short. In every decision, Michael seeks God's direction, whether it's through Scripture, quiet reflection, or speaking with trusted mentors in his faith community. This reliance on God helps him maintain a perspective of humility, reminding him that true strength and clarity come from God's sovereignty, not his own ability. By continually seeking God's presence in this challenging time, Michael remains grounded and avoids the temptation to handle things alone, knowing that his dependence on God is what will ultimately lead him through. This attitude not only strengthens his faith but also keeps his heart aligned with humility, recognizing that all breakthroughs and successes come by God's grace.

Small Prayer: Lord, I acknowledge my need for You in every aspect of my life. Help me to depend on Your strength and wisdom, keeping me humble and reliant on You. Amen.

End of the Week Closing Prayer for Spiritual Pride

"Dear Heavenly Father,

As I end this week, I come before You with a heart open to learning and growth. Thank You for revealing to me the ways that spiritual pride can subtly take root, and for guiding me in understanding how to guard against it. Help me, Lord, to remember the importance of full dependence on You. Remind me daily that all wisdom, strength, and grace come from You alone, and that without You, I am nothing.

Teach me to walk in humility, Lord. May I always approach my faith and relationships with a humble heart, knowing that You resist the proud but give grace to the humble. Show me how to be gentle and patient with others, never seeing myself as superior but rather as a servant, following the example of Christ.

This week, You've shown me the importance of serving others selflessly. Guide me to serve not for recognition or personal gain, but to bring Your love and light into the lives of others. Let every act of service reflect my gratitude to You, and remind me that my gifts and resources are meant to honor You, not to elevate myself.

Father, help me to recognize and confess any signs of spiritual pride within me. Let me be aware of moments when I may feel above correction, closed to learning, or tempted to compare myself with others. Guard my heart against the danger of comparison, so that I may focus only on my personal walk with You, free from envy or judgment.

Thank You, Lord, for Your grace, patience, and forgiveness. Help me to stay humble, dependent, and focused on You, so that my faith is genuine and my actions always reflect Your love. I ask that You continue to work within me, shaping my heart to be more like Christ.

In Jesus' name, Amen.".

Week 6: Spiritual Confusion

Introduction

Spiritual confusion involves feelings of uncertainty or doubt about one's spiritual path or beliefs. This condition can lead to a lack of direction and confidence in one's faith journey. The Bible provides guidance, encouragement, and clarity for those experiencing spiritual confusion, helping them to find firm footing in their relationship with God.

Definition: Spiritual Confusion: Uncertainty or doubt about one's spiritual path or beliefs.

Key Scriptures

James 1:5-6 (NIV) "If any of you lacks wisdom, you should ask God, who gives generously to all without finding fault, and it will be given to you. But when you ask, you must believe and not doubt, because the one who doubts is like a wave of the sea, blown and tossed by the wind."

Proverbs 3:5-6 (NIV) "Trust in the Lord with all your heart and lean not on your own understanding; in all your ways submit to him, and he will make your paths straight."

Psalm 119:105 (NIV) "Your word is a lamp for my feet, a light on my path."

1 Corinthians 14:33 (NIV) "For God is not a God of disorder but of peace—as in all the congregations of the Lord's people."

Isaiah 30:21 (NIV) "Whether you turn to the right or to the left, your ears will hear a voice behind you, saying, 'This is the way; walk in it.'"

Monday: Seeking Wisdom in Confusion

Explanation of Topic: When we're confused, it's natural to try to figure things out on our own. However, Scripture encourages us to seek wisdom from God, who understands all things. Spiritual confusion is an invitation to draw closer to Him for guidance.

Discussion Question: When you feel uncertain, what holds you back from seeking God's wisdom first? Is it fear that He may lead you in a direction you hadn't considered, a tendency to rely on your own understanding, or perhaps a lack of patience to wait for His guidance? Reflect on the reasons you might hesitate to turn to God initially and how these reasons might impact your relationship with Him. How might trusting God's wisdom over your own change the way you approach confusion? Consider how relying on His infinite knowledge, rather than your limited perspective, could bring a sense of peace and direction. Trusting in God's wisdom can help you release control, feel less overwhelmed, and approach situations with faith rather than anxiety. How might your outlook shift if you viewed confusion as an opportunity to deepen your dependence on God, allowing Him to guide you step by step?

Real-World Example: Emma has been offered an exciting job opportunity in another city—a position that perfectly aligns with her long-term career goals. Yet, the thought of moving away from her close friends, family, and familiar community leaves her feeling deeply conflicted. She knows this role could be a stepping stone in her career, but the idea of starting over in a new city brings a wave of uncertainty and anxiety. Initially, Emma tries to weigh the pros and cons on her own, endlessly analyzing what she might gain and what she stands to lose. Despite her efforts, she still feels torn, unable to find a clear answer. The confusion lingers, leaving her feeling emotionally drained and uncertain. Finally, Emma remembers the importance of seeking God's wisdom. She sets aside time for intentional prayer, asking God to guide her in making the best choice. As she continues to pray and reflect, Emma begins to feel a gradual sense of peace settle in her heart. While she doesn't have all the answers, she trusts that God will reveal the right path in His timing. Instead of wrestling with the decision alone, Emma finds comfort in knowing that God's wisdom surpasses her own understanding. This newfound peace helps her approach the decision with faith rather than fear, confident that God's guidance will lead her where she needs to be.

Small Prayer: "Lord, when I am confused, help me seek Your wisdom first. Give me a heart that trusts Your understanding over my own. Guide me to clarity, knowing that You are generous with wisdom. Amen."

Tuesday: Trusting God's Direction

Explanation of Topic: Trusting God when we can't see the path ahead can be challenging. Proverbs 3:5-6 reminds us to trust in God wholeheartedly and to submit to Him, even when we're unsure of the outcome.

Discussion Question: What parts of your life do you find hardest to surrender to God? Is it your career, relationships, finances, or future plans? Often, the areas we struggle to release are the ones where we feel most vulnerable, where outcomes matter deeply, and where we're afraid of losing control. Reflect on what makes it difficult to trust God fully in these areas. Do fears of failure, uncertainty, or disappointment hold you back from letting Him lead? How might releasing control and trusting His direction bring peace during times of confusion? Consider how surrendering allows you to rely on God's greater wisdom and perfect timing rather than the limits of your own understanding. Trusting God's direction can alleviate the stress of trying to have all the answers yourself, replacing anxiety with a sense of calm and faith. By letting go, you open yourself to God's guidance, which can lead to unexpected blessings and a deeper relationship with Him, bringing peace even in uncertain times.

Real-World Example: Real-World Example: David recently graduated and is stepping into a new phase of life, but he's feeling overwhelmed by the uncertainty of his future. Friends and family keep asking about his career plans, but he's unsure of his path and feels pressured to figure it all out quickly. Every time he sits down to make a plan, his mind races with questions: What if I choose the wrong career? What if I fail? The weight of these concerns only adds to his anxiety.

As he struggles to create a clear path forward, David realizes that he's been trying to handle everything on his own, relying on his own plans and expectations. He begins to wonder if he needs to approach this decision differently. In a moment of quiet reflection, David turns to prayer, asking God for guidance and peace. Over time, he begins to release his grip on his future, recognizing that God's plans may be different from his own. Through consistent prayer, David feels a sense of calm start to replace his anxiety. While he doesn't have all the answers, he finds comfort in knowing that he's not facing the unknown alone. By surrendering his future to God, David learns to trust that God will lead him one step at a time, giving him peace even in uncertainty.

Small Prayer: "Father, help me to trust You even when I can't see what's ahead. Teach me to surrender my plans to You and lean not on my own understanding. Direct my paths and give me peace. Amen."

Wednesday: Finding Guidance in God's Word

Explanation of Topic: God's Word is a source of light and guidance, especially in times of spiritual confusion. When we immerse ourselves in Scripture, God reveals His truth, which provides direction and dispels confusion.

Discussion Question: How often do you turn to Scripture when you're feeling lost or uncertain? Do you find yourself trying to navigate confusion through your own reasoning or seeking temporary solutions elsewhere? Reflect on how regularly immersing yourself in God's Word could provide clarity and direction during challenging times. Scripture is more than just words on a page; it is a source of divine wisdom, comfort, and truth. When we make it a habit to turn to God's Word, especially in moments of uncertainty, we allow His voice to guide us and illuminate the path forward. How might consistently seeking His Word help anchor your thoughts, align your heart with His will, and reduce the chaos of spiritual confusion? Consider how this practice could transform your perspective, replacing doubt with faith and confusion with confidence in God's promises.

Real-World Example: Sarah is faced with a major decision that will significantly impact her family's future. She spends countless hours researching her options, seeking advice, and weighing the pros and cons. Despite her best efforts, she remains conflicted, unable to find clarity. The uncertainty begins to weigh on her, leaving her feeling anxious and stuck. One evening, after another fruitless day of searching for answers, Sarah decides to pause and turn to God's Word for guidance. She opens her Bible and reads Psalm 119:105: "Your word is a lamp for my feet, a light on my path." The verse speaks deeply to her heart, reminding her that God's Word provides clarity and direction when her own understanding falls short. Encouraged by this truth, Sarah continues to spend time in Scripture and prayer each day, allowing God's Word to guide her decisions. While she still doesn't have all the answers, she begins to feel a sense of peace knowing that God is illuminating the next steps, even if the entire path isn't clear yet. By turning to Scripture, Sarah finds the confidence to trust God's direction and move forward with faith rather than fear.

Small Prayer: "Lord, thank You for the guidance of Your Word. Help me to remember that Your Word is a lamp for my feet and a light for my path. Let Your truth guide me when I am uncertain. Amen."

Thursday: Accepting God's Higher Ways

Explanation of Topic: Spiritual confusion often arises because we don't understand God's ways. Isaiah 55:8-9 teaches us that God's thoughts are higher than ours, reminding us to trust Him even when we don't fully understand.

Discussion Question: How do you typically respond when God's plans differ from your expectations or hopes? Do you find yourself resisting His direction, asking why things aren't going as planned, or doubting His goodness and purpose? Consider how these reactions might reveal a desire for control or an inability to fully trust in God's sovereignty.

How might accepting that God's ways are infinitely higher than yours bring peace and trust, even when the circumstances are unclear? Reflect on how surrendering your limited understanding to God's infinite wisdom can shift your perspective. When you trust that His plans are for your ultimate good, even when they don't align with your own, how might that change your ability to face uncertainty with faith rather than fear? Consider how this act of surrender can transform disappointment into an opportunity to grow closer to God and rely on His perfect timing and guidance.

Real-World Example: Tom had always approached life with a detailed plan, setting clear goals and timelines for his career, relationships, and personal achievements. For years, his plans seemed to unfold smoothly, reinforcing his belief that careful preparation was the key to success. But then, unexpected challenges disrupted his carefully laid path—a job opportunity he was sure he'd secure fell through, a long-term relationship ended unexpectedly, and unforeseen financial struggles emerged. These setbacks left Tom feeling disoriented and questioning why things weren't going as he hoped. He began to doubt whether God was truly guiding his steps or if his prayers for direction had gone unheard. In his frustration, Tom tried harder to regain control, but the more he pushed, the more overwhelmed he felt. One evening, while reading his Bible, he came across Isaiah 55:8-9: "For my thoughts are not your thoughts, neither are your ways my ways," declares the Lord. The verse resonated deeply, reminding him that God's plans and perspective are far greater than his own. Tom realized he had been relying too heavily on his understanding and not trusting God's infinite wisdom. Instead of resisting, Tom began to pray for peace and the ability to surrender his plans to God. Over time, he found comfort in the assurance that God's ways, though different from his own, were ultimately for his good. This shift in perspective allowed him to approach his challenges with faith rather than fear, trusting that God was working behind the scenes to lead him to something even better than he could have planned.

Small Prayer: "Lord, help me accept that Your ways are higher than mine. When I don't understand, teach me to trust that Your plans are better. Let me find peace in knowing You see the bigger picture. Amen."

Friday: Finding Peace in God, Not Confusion

Explanation of Topic: Spiritual confusion doesn't come from God, who is a God of peace. When we feel overwhelmed by doubts and uncertainties, we can rest in God's promise of peace, trusting that He will lead us away from confusion.

Discussion Question: In moments of spiritual confusion, do you find yourself actively seeking God's peace, or do you become consumed by doubt and the need to figure everything out on your own? Reflect on how doubt can create a cycle of anxiety, making it harder to hear God's voice or trust His presence. Consider how this impacts your ability to move forward with faith and confidence. How might focusing on God's peace help you find clarity? God's peace is not the absence of uncertainty but the assurance of His presence and guidance in the midst of it. By anchoring your heart in His peace, you can quiet the noise of fear and doubt, creating space for His wisdom to direct your steps. Reflect on how trusting in God's character and promises can shift your perspective, allowing clarity and calm to replace the confusion that often accompanies spiritual struggles.

Real-World Example: Lisa is facing a major life decision that could significantly impact her future. Despite spending hours researching, consulting friends, and analyzing her options, she feels paralyzed by confusion and anxiety. The weight of the decision leaves her restless, and she starts doubting her ability to make the right choice. Her thoughts spiral, and she begins to feel overwhelmed by the chaos in her mind. In her frustration, Lisa turns to her Bible, seeking comfort and guidance. She comes across 1 Corinthians 14:33: "For God is not a God of confusion but of peace." The verse strikes her deeply, reminding her that the anxiety she's feeling doesn't come from God. Instead, His nature is one of peace and clarity. Inspired by this truth, Lisa decides to pause her frantic efforts and bring her decision to God in prayer. As she prays, she asks God to replace her anxiety with His peace and to guide her heart as she listens for His direction. Over time, Lisa begins to feel a calming presence, even though the decision isn't fully resolved. She realizes that trusting in God's peace allows her to approach the situation with faith rather than fear. By focusing on God's nature and promises, Lisa finds the strength to let go of her doubts, trusting that He will guide her step by step.

Small Prayer: "God of peace, remind me that confusion is not from You. Fill my heart with Your peace and help me to rely on Your guidance. Bring me clarity and calm in times of doubt. Amen."

End of the Week Closing Prayer for Spiritual Confusion

Dear Heavenly Father,

Thank You for walking with me through this week as I explored the journey of spiritual confusion. Thank You for reminding me of the importance of seeking Your wisdom when I feel uncertain and trusting in Your direction over my own. I am grateful for Your Word, which lights my path, guiding me when I feel lost. Help me to embrace Your higher ways, knowing that You see what I cannot and that Your plans are perfect. Lord, I am grateful for the reminder that You are not a God of confusion but of peace. Let this truth anchor me in times of doubt and fear. Fill my heart with Your peace and help me to seek You wholeheartedly. As I move forward, teach me to trust You more deeply and lean into Your guidance, knowing that You are always with me, leading me with love and wisdom.

In Jesus' name, Amen.

Week 7: Spiritual Anger

Introduction

Spiritual anger is a feeling of resentment, frustration, or bitterness directed toward God, faith, or spiritual beliefs, often stemming from unmet expectations, pain, or confusion. This week, we'll explore how spiritual anger manifests, what Scripture teaches us about it, and how we can overcome it through prayer, reflection, and surrender to God's grace.

Definition: Spiritual Anger: A state of emotional and spiritual turmoil where feelings of frustration, resentment, or bitterness arise in response to perceived injustices, unanswered prayers, or personal suffering, often causing a strain in one's relationship with God.

Key Scriptures

Psalm 13:1-2 (NIV) "How long, Lord? Will you forget me forever? How long will you hide your face from me? How long must I wrestle with my thoughts and day after day have sorrow in my heart? How long will my enemy triumph over me?"

Ephesians 4:26-27 (NIV) In your anger do not sin: Do not let the sun go down while you are still angry, and do not give the devil a foothold."

James 1:19-20 (NIV) My dear brothers and sisters, take note of this: Everyone should be quick to listen, slow to speak and slow to become angry, because human anger does not produce the righteousness that God desires."

Romans 12:19 (NIV) Do not take revenge, my dear friends, but leave room for God's wrath, for it is written: 'It is mine to avenge; I will repay,' says the Lord."

Romans 8:28 (NIV) And we know that in all things God works for the good of those who love him, who have been called according to his purpose."

Psalm 37:8-9 (NIV) Refrain from anger and turn from wrath; do not fret—it leads only to evil. For those who are evil will be destroyed, but those who hope in the Lord will inherit the land."

Monday: Recognizing Spiritual Anger

Explanation of Topic: Begin by acknowledging your feelings of anger. Denying or suppressing these emotions only deepens their impact. Recognizing spiritual anger is the first step toward healing.

Discussion Question: Reflect on a time when you felt anger toward God. What specific situation or event triggered this emotion? Was it a loss, an unanswered prayer, or a season of pain or disappointment? Consider how these feelings influenced your faith—did they create distance between you and God, or did they lead you to wrestle with your understanding of His character? Think about your actions during that time. Did you withdraw from prayer, worship, or community, or did you try to seek answers or comfort in other ways? Reflecting on these moments can reveal how anger impacts your spiritual journey and how God's presence and grace can guide you toward healing.

Real-World Example: Emma had been praying fervently for stability in her life, especially in her job, which was her primary source of security. When she was unexpectedly laid off, the shock and frustration were overwhelming. She couldn't understand why God would allow such a thing to happen when she had been seeking His guidance and provision. This led to a deep sense of anger toward God, as Emma felt her prayers had gone unanswered. Her frustration caused her to pull back from prayer and church, leaving her feeling distant from God and unsure about her faith. Emma's confusion grew as she wrestled with the tension between her trust in God's promises and the reality of her situation.

Small Prayer: "Lord, help me to recognize my anger and bring it to You honestly. Teach me to trust that You can handle my emotions and guide me toward peace. Amen.

Tuesday: Understanding the Root of Anger

Explanation of Topic: Spiritual anger often stems from unmet expectations, pain, or a sense of injustice. Understanding its root helps us address it effectively.

Discussion Question: Reflect on any unmet expectations or painful experiences in your life that may have stirred feelings of anger or frustration toward God. Was it a specific prayer that went unanswered, a loss that felt unfair, or a season of struggle where God seemed distant? How have these experiences shaped your view of God and your relationship with Him? Consider what it would look like to fully surrender these feelings to Him—acknowledging your hurt, trusting His greater plan, and inviting His healing into those areas of your life. How might letting go of these burdens transform your faith and bring you closer to God?

Real-World Example: John was devastated when his loved one passed away after a long illness. He had prayed fervently for healing, pleading with God to spare their life. When his prayers seemed to go unanswered, John was overwhelmed with a sense of betrayal and confusion. He couldn't understand why God, who he believed was loving and all-powerful, would allow such a loss. This pain turned into anger, creating a barrier in his relationship with God. John found it difficult to pray or read Scripture, as his grief and unanswered questions left him feeling distant and abandoned. His anger became a way of coping with his deep sorrow, though it also left him wrestling with doubts about his faith.

Small Prayer: "Lord, reveal the roots of my anger so I may bring them to You. Heal the wounds that fuel my frustration and teach me to trust in Your greater plan. Amen."

Wednesday: Confronting Anger with Scripture

Explanation of Topic: The Bible offers wisdom for addressing anger. Reflecting on God's Word helps to replace bitterness with understanding and trust.

Discussion Question: Reflect on the guidance offered in Scriptures like Ephesians 4:26, which says, "In your anger, do not sin: Do not let the sun go down while you are still angry," and Psalm 37:8, which urges us to "Refrain from anger and turn from wrath; do not fret—it leads only to evil." How do these verses challenge you to examine your response to anger? Consider how they remind us that anger itself is not sinful, but unchecked anger can lead us away from God's will. What practical steps can you take to manage your anger in a way that aligns with God's desires? This could include pausing to pray, seeking wisdom in Scripture, or speaking with a trusted mentor. How might intentionally surrendering your anger to God help transform it into peace and spiritual growth?

Real-World Example: Lisa faced a long and challenging season of illness that left her feeling abandoned and frustrated. She had prayed endlessly for healing but saw no change in her condition, which deepened her anger and sense of isolation from God. One day, a friend encouraged her to reflect on Psalm 37:8, which says, "Refrain from anger and turn from wrath; do not fret—it leads only to evil." At first, Lisa struggled to connect with the verse, feeling that her emotions were justified given her circumstances. However, as she continued to meditate on the Scripture daily, she began to feel its truth sinking into her heart. She realized that holding onto anger was only adding to her pain and creating a barrier between her and God. Over time, these reflections softened her heart and reminded her of God's constant presence, even in her suffering. Lisa found comfort in the knowledge that God was with her, transforming her anger into trust and her frustration into peace, even as her circumstances remained unchanged.

Small Prayer: "Father, let Your Word transform my heart. Teach me to release my anger and replace it with trust in Your wisdom and timing. Amen."

Thursday: Releasing Anger Through Forgiveness

Explanation of Topic: Holding onto anger, even toward God, can harden our hearts. Forgiveness allows us to release the weight of resentment and renew our relationship with Him.

Discussion Question: What does it mean to forgive God, even though He is blameless and perfect in all His ways? While God does no wrong, our limited understanding of His plans and purposes can lead to feelings of hurt, disappointment, or betrayal. Forgiving God doesn't mean He has done something wrong, but it signifies our willingness to release the anger, resentment, or misunderstandings we may be holding against Him. It's an act of surrender, acknowledging that His ways are higher than ours and that He is working for our good, even when we don't see it. How might letting go of these emotions open your heart to healing, renew your faith, and restore your trust in His sovereignty?

Real-World Example: Michael and his wife had endured years of infertility struggles, facing countless doctor appointments, failed treatments, and emotional heartache. Each passing year without an answer to their prayers for a child deepened Michael's bitterness toward God. He wrestled with questions of fairness and felt abandoned, wondering why God seemed silent in their time of greatest need. This resentment began to weigh heavily on his faith, creating a sense of distance from God and a growing hopelessness in his heart.

After a candid conversation with a trusted mentor, Michael realized that his anger and unforgiveness toward God were preventing him from experiencing peace and spiritual renewal. While he acknowledged that God had not wronged him, Michael understood the importance of releasing his resentment. Through prayer and reflection on Scripture, he chose to forgive God—not as an admission of fault on God's part, but as a way to let go of the bitterness that was holding him captive.

As Michael released his anger, he began to feel a renewed sense of peace and trust in God's plan. Though the pain of unanswered prayers remained, he found comfort in knowing that God's love and sovereignty were unchanging. Michael's act of surrender transformed his perspective, allowing him to embrace faith and hope, even in the midst of uncertainty. This shift not only strengthened his relationship with God but also deepened his resilience as he continued his journey of trusting in God's timing.

Small Prayer: "Lord, I release my anger to You and choose forgiveness. Help me to let go of bitterness and embrace the peace that only You can provide. Amen."

Friday: Trusting God's Sovereignty

Explanation: Overcoming spiritual anger requires surrendering to God's sovereignty, trusting that His plans are greater than our understanding.

Discussion Question: How can trusting in God's sovereignty help you find peace in the midst of unanswered prayers or difficult circumstances? Trusting in God's sovereignty means believing that He is in control, that His plans are higher than ours, and that He is working all things for our ultimate good, even when we don't understand. Unanswered prayers or unexpected hardships can lead to frustration, doubt, or anger, but trusting in God's greater purpose shifts our focus from why something is happening to who is guiding us through it.

When we surrender our need for immediate answers and lean on God's wisdom, we begin to find peace, knowing that He sees the full picture while we only see a part. His timing is perfect, and His ways are intentional, even if they don't align with our expectations. Reflect on how embracing this truth can bring comfort during seasons of pain or confusion. How might trusting that God is sovereign help you let go of fear, control, or resentment and instead find rest in His unfailing love and promises?

Real-World Example: Sarah had poured her time, money, and energy into building her dream business, but despite her hard work, it ultimately failed. She felt devastated, angry, and confused, questioning why God would allow such a painful setback after she had prayed for success and guidance. Her feelings of frustration led her to believe that her efforts had been wasted, and her faith began to waver as she struggled to see any purpose in her failure.

One day, a friend shared Romans 8:28 with her: "And we know that in all things God works for the good of those who love Him, who have been called according to His purpose." Sarah began to meditate on this verse daily, slowly shifting her focus from what she had lost to what God might be teaching her. As she surrendered her anger and disappointment, she realized that even in failure, God was working to shape her character, build resilience, and prepare her for something greater.

This truth brought her a sense of peace and renewed trust in God's sovereignty. While the business had ended, Sarah's faith grew stronger, and she began to see the experience as part of her journey rather than the end of it. Trusting God's plan gave her the courage to move forward, knowing that He could use even her struggles for His greater purpose.

Small Prayer: "Lord, I trust in Your sovereignty and Your plans for my life. Help me to see Your hand at work, even in my struggles, and to rest in Your perfect wisdom. Amen."

End of the Week Closing Prayer: Spiritual Anger

Heavenly Father,

We come before you acknowledging the anger and resentment that weigh on our hearts. We confess that at times, we have allowed these emotions to distance us from You and from others. Lord, teach us to bring our frustrations honestly to You, knowing that You can handle our deepest hurts and questions. Help us to trust in Your justice and your perfect timing, even when we cannot see the full picture.

Father, shape us to reflect Your character—slow to anger, quick to listen, and eager to extend grace. Give us the courage to resolve conflicts quickly and to forgive as You have forgiven us. Let Your Word be a lamp that guides us toward peace, reconciliation, and renewed faith. Transform our anger into opportunities to grow closer to You, to build humility, and to reflect Your love in our actions.

We thank you for your endless patience and mercy, and we ask that You fill us with Your peace as we surrender our struggles to You. In Jesus' name, we pray. Amen.

Week 8: Spiritual Fatigue

Introduction

Spiritual fatigue is a state of emotional and spiritual exhaustion that can leave us feeling disconnected from God, drained of purpose, and weary in our faith journey. This week, we'll explore the causes of spiritual fatigue, what Scripture teaches us about renewing our strength, and practical steps to find rest, refreshment, and revival in God's presence.

Definition

Spiritual Fatigue: A state of weariness or burnout that occurs when our spiritual life feels stagnant or overwhelming, often caused by unbalanced expectations, prolonged struggles, or a lack of connection with God.

Key Scriptures

Matthew 11:28-30 "Come to me, all you who are weary and burdened, and I will give you rest. Take my yoke upon you and learn from me, for I am gentle and humble in heart, and you will find rest for your souls. For my yoke is easy and my burden is light.

Isaiah 40:31 "But those who hope in the Lord will renew their strength. They will soar on wings like eagles; they will run and not grow weary, they will walk and not be faint."

Galatians 6:9 Let us not grow weary in doing good, for at the proper time we will reap harvest if we do not give up."

Psalm 23:3 "He refreshes my soul. He guides me along the right paths for His name's sake."

Corinthians 12:9 But he said to me, 'My grace is sufficient for you, for my power is made perfect in weakness.' Therefore I will boast all the more gladly of my weaknesses, so that the power of Christ may rest upon me." ."

Discussion Questions

Monday: Recognizing Spiritual Fatigue

Explanation: The first step in addressing spiritual fatigue is to recognize its symptoms. These can include feeling disconnected from God, losing motivation for prayer or worship, or feeling overwhelmed by life's demands.

Discussion Question: Reflect on a time when you felt spiritually drained. What were the specific signs that revealed this fatigue—did you feel distant from God, struggle to pray, or lose motivation for reading Scripture and worship? Perhaps you found yourself going through the motions without joy or meaning, or life's challenges felt heavier than usual. How did this spiritual weariness impact your relationship with God? Did it cause you to pull away from Him, question His presence, or stop seeking Him altogether?

Also, consider how it affected your interactions with others. Were you more irritable, withdrawn, or less willing to offer support and love to those around you? Spiritual fatigue can create isolation, making us feel alone in our struggles. Reflect on how acknowledging this fatigue and intentionally seeking God's renewal could have helped restore both your connection with Him and your relationships with others. What lessons can you take from that experience to recognize and address spiritual fatigue more effectively in the future?

Real-World Example: Sarah was known in her church as someone who was always ready to serve—volunteering in children's ministry, helping with events, and attending every small group session. Her days were filled with church commitments, and she felt proud of how much she was contributing to her faith community. However, over time, Sarah began to notice a shift. Her once vibrant spiritual life started to feel mechanical, as though she was simply checking off boxes. Prayer felt empty, worship became routine, and her connection with God felt distant.

The more she poured herself into serving, the more exhausted and unfulfilled she felt. Her commitments, though good, had taken the place of quiet time with God and personal reflection. Sarah began to feel overwhelmed and spiritually dry, questioning why her efforts no longer brought her the joy and passion they once had. This spiritual fatigue affected her relationships as well—she became irritable and withdrawn, unable to give her family or friends the attention they deserved.

One day, after an emotional conversation with a trusted mentor, Sarah realized she had been so busy "doing" for God that she had neglected simply being with Him. She decided to take a step back, setting aside time each day to pray, rest, and immerse herself in Scripture without any agenda. Slowly, her passion for her faith reignited. By prioritizing her personal relationship with God, Sarah learned that true spiritual fulfillment comes not from constant activity but from quiet moments in His presence. This shift allowed her to serve others again, but now with a heart renewed and strengthened by God's grace.

Small Prayer: "Lord, help me to recognize the areas of my life where I feel spiritually drained. Open my heart to Your presence and renew my strength. Amen."

Tuesday: The Causes of Spiritual Fatigue

Explanation: Spiritual fatigue can arise from many sources, such as overcommitment, unbalanced expectations, prolonged trials, or neglecting personal time with God. Identifying the cause helps us take steps toward renewal.

Discussion Question: Reflect on your life and identify specific circumstances or habits that may have led to spiritual fatigue. Were there seasons when you felt overwhelmed by responsibilities at work, church, or home? Perhaps you overcommitted to serving others while neglecting your personal time with God. Were there prolonged struggles, such as financial difficulties, health issues, or relational conflicts, that drained your emotional and spiritual energy? Consider if habits like prioritizing busyness over prayer, neglecting rest, or relying on your own strength rather than seeking God's help played a role.

How has this fatigue impacted your relationship with God—did it create distance, make prayer feel like a chore, or cause you to lose motivation for spiritual growth? Reflect on practical steps you can take to address these causes with God's guidance. Could you set aside intentional time for rest, reconnect through daily prayer or Scripture, or simplify your commitments to focus on what truly nourishes your soul? How can trusting God's strength, rather than your own, help you overcome the weariness you feel? What might it look like to surrender these burdens to Him and allow Him to refresh your spirit?

Real-World Example: Michael had been searching for a new job for months after an unexpected layoff. Each day felt like a battle as he scoured job boards, sent out resumes, and prepared for interviews, only to face rejection after rejection. His financial concerns grew heavier with every passing week, and he began to feel the pressure of providing for his family. Determined to solve the problem on his own, Michael threw himself into his efforts, neglecting time for prayer, reflection, or rest.

As the stress piled up, Michael began to notice changes in himself. His prayers became hurried or nonexistent, and he felt too exhausted to read his Bible. The peace he once found in God's presence was replaced by feelings of frustration and weariness. Michael became short-tempered with his family and withdrawn from his church community, which left him feeling isolated and unsupported.

It wasn't until a close friend asked how he was doing spiritually that Michael realized the depth of his spiritual fatigue. The friend encouraged him to bring his struggles to God, reminding him of Matthew 11:28: "Come to me, all you who are weary and burdened, and I will give you rest." That night, Michael poured out his worries to God in prayer, admitting that he had been trying to carry the weight alone. Over time, he began to trust God's timing and provision, allowing himself to rest in the knowledge that God was in control. Though the job search continued, Michael felt renewed strength and peace, no longer striving in his own power but relying on God's guidance and grace.

Small Prayer: "Lord, show me the causes of my spiritual fatigue and guide me in releasing these burdens to You. Teach me to trust in Your care. Amen."

Wednesday: Finding Rest in God

Explanation: True rest comes from surrendering our burdens to God and trusting in His care. Through prayer, reflection, and time in His presence, we can find the spiritual refreshment we need.

Discussion Question: What does it mean to find rest in God? Finding rest in God goes beyond physical relaxation; it is a spiritual and emotional peace that comes from trusting Him completely. It means stepping away from striving, worry, and the need to control outcomes, and instead placing your burdens into His capable hands. This rest is not just about inactivity but about actively seeking God—turning to Him in prayer, meditating on His Word, and trusting His promises. It is a place where you can lay down your anxieties, knowing that God is sovereign, loving, and faithful.

Consider how surrendering your worries to God can renew your soul. When you hold onto fear, stress, or frustration, it drains you spiritually and emotionally. However, when you intentionally take time to sit in God's presence, even in silence, He refreshes you with His peace. Scripture promises this in Matthew 11:28: "Come to me, all you who are weary and burdened, and I will give you rest." Reflect on how moments of prayer, worship, or quiet reflection have helped you release your burdens in the past.

What would it look like in your life right now to spend intentional time with God each day? How might it change your outlook on your challenges, your relationships, and your faith? Finding rest in God doesn't mean all your problems disappear, but it allows you to approach life with renewed strength, peace, and trust, knowing He is walking with you.

Real-World Example: Emma, a mother of three young children, found herself constantly overwhelmed by the demands of her busy life. Between caring for her kids, managing household chores, and juggling part-time work, she felt like there was never a moment to catch her breath. Every day blurred into the next, leaving her emotionally drained, physically exhausted, and spiritually disconnected. She began to notice her patience running thin and her joy slipping away, which weighed heavily on her heart. She felt guilty for feeling this way but didn't know how to fix it.

One day, after confiding in a friend, Emma was encouraged to set aside just a few minutes each morning for quiet time with God. At first, it felt impossible to carve out any time for herself, but she decided to try. Each morning, before her children woke up, Emma sat with her Bible, prayed, and listened to worship music. In those moments of stillness, she poured out her worries to God and meditated on Scriptures like Matthew 11:28: "Come to me, all you who are weary and burdened, and I will give you rest."

Over time, these small moments of intentional connection with God began to transform her outlook. Though her circumstances didn't change—her responsibilities were still many—Emma felt a renewed sense of peace and strength that carried her through the day. She realized that finding rest in God wasn't about escaping her life's demands but about letting God's presence refresh and strengthen her spirit. By surrendering her burdens to Him, Emma felt less overwhelmed and more equipped to face each day with gratitude and hope.

Prayer: "Lord, I come to You with my burdens and ask for Your rest. Refresh my soul and remind me of the peace found in Your presence. Amen."

Thursday: Relying on God's Strength

Explanation: Spiritual fatigue often reminds us of our limitations and the need to rely on God's strength rather than our own. His grace is sufficient to carry us through when we feel weak.

Discussion Question: How can relying on God's strength, instead of your own, transform the way you handle your struggles? When we rely solely on our own abilities, we often end up feeling overwhelmed, frustrated, or even defeated. Our strength is limited, and trying to carry heavy burdens alone can lead to burnout and spiritual fatigue. However, when we choose to lean on God's strength, we tap into a limitless source of power, grace, and wisdom. This shift allows us to face challenges with greater peace and confidence, knowing we're not alone.

Reflect on specific areas in your life where you've tried to handle things on your own. How might inviting God into those situations change your perspective and give you the endurance to keep going? Consider practical steps to depend more on His power daily. This might include starting your day with prayer, asking for His guidance before making decisions, meditating on Scriptures like 2 Corinthians 12:9 ("My grace is sufficient for you, for my power is made perfect in weakness"), or taking moments throughout the day to pause and surrender your worries to Him.

What would it look like to live each day trusting in God's strength rather than striving in your own? How might this dependence lead to a deeper relationship with Him and a greater sense of peace in the midst of your struggles?

Real-World Example: John, a dedicated high school teacher and father of two, found himself stretched to his limits. Between preparing lesson plans, grading assignments, attending parent-teacher conferences, and spending time with his family, he felt utterly exhausted. The demands of his job left little energy for his personal life, and his relationship with God began to feel like an afterthought. Over time, John's exhaustion turned into frustration. He felt as though he was failing both at work and at home, and the weight of it all seemed too much to bear.

One evening, after a particularly exhausting day, John stumbled upon 2 Corinthians 12:9: "My grace is sufficient for you, for my power is made perfect in weakness." The verse struck a chord with him, and he realized that he had been trying to manage everything on his own instead of seeking God's strength. That night, he knelt in prayer, pouring out his feelings of inadequacy and asking God to sustain him.

The next morning, John began a new habit. Before starting his day, he spent a few quiet minutes in prayer, asking God for wisdom, patience, and strength. This simple practice became a daily routine, and though his schedule didn't change, John noticed something profound. He felt a renewed sense of energy and peace that he couldn't explain. Tasks that once felt overwhelming became manageable, and his interactions with students and family became more patient and intentional.

John realized that depending on God's strength didn't mean his struggles would disappear, but it gave him the grace to face them with confidence and calm. By surrendering his exhaustion to God each day, he found a sense of balance and hope that transformed both his work and family life.

Small Prayer: "Lord, remind me that Your grace is sufficient for my every need. Teach me to depend on Your strength when I feel weak. Amen."

Friday: Persevering with Hope

Explanation: Spiritual fatigue doesn't mean the end of your faith journey. By holding onto hope, trusting God's promises, and staying connected to Him, you can persevere and experience renewal.

Discussion Question: How can trusting in God's promises and focusing on hope help you push through seasons of spiritual fatigue? Spiritual fatigue often feels like wandering through a dry, empty place, where prayer feels hollow and faith feels distant. During these times, God's promises remind us that He is faithful, present, and working even when we can't see it. Scriptures like Isaiah 40:31—"But those who hope in the Lord will renew their strength"—give us the assurance that God will sustain us and restore our spiritual energy when we lean on Him.

Reflect on how clinging to God's promises can shift your focus from weariness to trust. Instead of dwelling on your limitations or circumstances, His Word offers hope that He will carry you through, no matter how tired or discouraged you feel. Think back to past seasons in your life when you felt spiritually drained but experienced renewal. What brought you through those moments? Was it a time of prayer, encouragement from others, worship, or a specific Scripture? How did God show His faithfulness during that time, even when it was hard to see?

Reflecting on God's past work in your life can strengthen your confidence that He will do it again. His promises are unchanging, and placing your hope in Him allows you to persevere, knowing that spiritual renewal will come in His timing. How can you remind yourself of His faithfulness today, trusting that even in seasons of fatigue, God is at work and His hope will not fail you?

Real-World Example: Lisa had been feeling spiritually dry for months. Her prayers felt empty, reading the Bible seemed like a chore, and worship no longer brought her the joy it once did. She couldn't pinpoint exactly when the spiritual fatigue started, but the weight of daily struggles—work stress, family obligations, and personal disappointments—had slowly drained her spirit. She began to feel disconnected from God, questioning if He was listening or even cared.

One afternoon, overwhelmed by this emptiness, Lisa sat quietly in her living room and began reflecting on her faith journey. As she thought back, she remembered a time when she had faced a particularly difficult struggle—an unexpected loss that had left her devastated. During that season, Lisa recalled how God had met her in her pain. She remembered the peace He brought through prayer, the strength she felt after reading promises in Scripture, and the support He provided through friends and family. Though that season had been difficult, God's presence had carried her through, restoring her joy and faith.

This memory stirred something deep in Lisa's heart. She realized that the same God who had been faithful before was still with her now, even in her dryness. Encouraged by this reminder, she began to seek Him intentionally once again. Lisa opened her Bible to Psalm 23:3: "He refreshes my soul. He guides me along the right paths for His name's sake." She meditated on those words, allowing them to remind her that God could and would restore her soul. Slowly, Lisa felt a renewed sense of hope and determination to pursue God's presence, trusting in His promises to bring her strength and joy once more. This shift in perspective gave her the courage to keep seeking Him, even when it felt hard, knowing He was working to renew her spirit just as He had in the past.

Small Prayer: "Lord, give me the hope and perseverance to continue seeking You, even in moments of weariness. Fill my heart with the assurance of Your faithfulness. Amen."

End of the Week Closing Prayer: Spiritual Fatigue

"Dear Heavenly Father,

Thank You for walking with me through this week as I faced my spiritual fatigue. I bring to You my weariness, my struggles, and my feelings of disconnection, knowing that You are my source of rest and renewal. Teach me to recognize the signs of fatigue and the habits or circumstances that contribute to it. Help me to find true rest in You, surrendering my burdens and trusting in Your care.

Lord, remind me daily that Your strength is made perfect in my weakness, and Your grace is sufficient for me. When I feel discouraged, help me to persevere with hope, trusting in Your promises and Your plan for my life. Thank You for refreshing my soul and guiding me along the right paths.

Week 9: Overcoming Spiritual Envy

Introduction

Spiritual envy occurs when we feel jealousy or resentment toward others' spiritual gifts, experiences, or progress. This emotion can cause discontentment, bitterness, and even damage to our spiritual relationships. The Bible provides wisdom to help us overcome envy and instead cultivate gratitude, humility, and contentment in our walk with God. By focusing on our unique journey and God's diverse work in the lives of others, we can build a spirit of unity and love within the body of Christ.

Definition

Spiritual Envy: Jealousy or resentment toward others' spiritual experiences, gifts, or growth, leading to discontentment and distraction from one's own relationship with God.

Key Scriptures

James 3:14-16 (NIV): "But if you harbor bitter envy and selfish ambition in your hearts, do not boast about it or deny the truth. Such 'wisdom' does not come down from heaven but is earthly, unspiritual, demonic. For where you have envy and selfish ambition, there you find disorder and every evil practice."

Galatians 5:25-26 (NIV): "Since we live by the Spirit, let us keep in step with the Spirit. Let us not become conceited, provoking and envying each other."

1 Corinthians 12:4-6 (NIV): "There are different kinds of gifts, but the same Spirit distributes them. There are different kinds of service, but the same Lord. There are different kinds of working, but in all of them and in everyone it is the same God at work."

Romans 12:15 (NIV): "Rejoice with those who rejoice; mourn with those who mourn."

Philippians 2:3-4 (NIV): "Do nothing out of selfish ambition or vain conceit. Rather, in humility value others above yourselves, not looking to your own interests but each of you to the interests of the others."

Monday: Recognizing the Dangers of Envy

Explanation of Topic: Envy, as described in James 3:14-16, leads to disorder and spiritual discontentment. It shifts our focus from God to comparison, creating unnecessary bitterness and division.

Discussion Question: How does harboring envy affect your spiritual life, your focus on God, and your relationships with others? Envy, at its core, shifts your attention away from God's blessings and purpose for your life and onto what others have. This can create a sense of discontentment, causing you to question God's goodness and His plan for you. Spiritually, envy erodes your trust in God, making it difficult to fully rely on Him or celebrate His work in your life. It may also lead to bitterness or resentment, creating a barrier in your relationship with God.

Envy not only impacts your spiritual focus but also strains your relationships with others. When you harbor envy, you may find it harder to rejoice in others' successes or growth, which can foster jealousy, competition, or even hostility. These feelings disrupt the unity and love that God calls us to cultivate in our communities. Instead of building up others, envy can lead to comparison and judgment, further distancing you from healthy, Christ-centered relationships.

Reflect on how envy has influenced your actions or mindset in the past. Did it make you less grateful for your blessings or hinder your ability to connect with others authentically? What practical steps can you take to address these feelings and refocus your heart on God? Consider how cultivating gratitude, prayer, and humility can help you overcome envy and restore both your spiritual life and your relationships. How might trusting in God's unique plan for you free you from the grip of envy and bring peace to your heart?

Real-World Example: Emily, a young and passionate believer, was actively involved in her church. She loved participating in ministry and had always dreamed of taking on a leadership role. However, when her close friend Sarah was appointed to a position Emily had hoped for, she couldn't help but feel a pang of jealousy. Though she congratulated Sarah outwardly, inwardly Emily struggled with bitterness. She began questioning why God had chosen Sarah for the role and not her, even though she believed she was equally committed and capable.

As time went on, Emily's envy grew, making it difficult for her to fully support or celebrate Sarah's success. She found herself avoiding conversations with Sarah and withdrawing from group activities where Sarah was leading. This isolation left Emily feeling disconnected from her friend, her church community, and even God. She began doubting her own worth and purpose, which only deepened her frustration.

Small Prayer: Lord, help me to recognize the destructive nature of envy. Teach me to confess these feelings and find contentment in Your plans for my life. Amen.

Tuesday: Walking in Step with the Spirit

Explanation of Topic: Living by the Spirit requires rejecting envy and trusting in God's unique work in our lives. This focus brings joy and contentment, aligning us with His purpose.

Discussion Question: In what ways does Galatians 5:25-26 challenge you to reject envy and live by the Spirit's guidance? This passage, which says, "Since we live by the Spirit, let us keep in step with the Spirit. Let us not become conceited, provoking and envying each other," reminds us that walking in the Spirit requires a conscious rejection of envy and selfish ambition. Envy shifts our focus away from God's work in our lives and places it on comparisons with others, leading to discontentment, division, and spiritual stagnation.

Living by the Spirit means aligning your thoughts, actions, and desires with God's will rather than the fleeting standards of the world. The Spirit's guidance encourages you to trust God's unique plan for your life and to celebrate the blessings He gives to others without comparison.

This requires humility and gratitude, as well as a commitment to replace jealousy with love and encouragement for others.

Reflect on how envy might have influenced your thoughts or actions in the past. Have you ever felt frustrated or inadequate because you compared your journey to someone else's? How did those feelings affect your relationship with God and your ability to trust Him fully? Consider the practical steps you can take to reject envy and keep in step with the Spirit—such as praying for contentment, meditating on Scripture, or intentionally celebrating others' successes. How might surrendering your envy to God free you to focus on your own spiritual growth and deepen your connection with Him?

Real-World Example: Mark had been a member of his church for several years, but he often found himself comparing his spiritual journey to those around him. He admired others who seemed to pray with more eloquence, quote Scripture effortlessly, or lead ministries with confidence. These comparisons left Mark feeling inadequate, as though his contributions to the church and his personal growth weren't enough. He began doubting his own faith, questioning why he wasn't progressing as quickly or visibly as others.

Mark's feelings of inferiority grew to the point where he hesitated to volunteer for new opportunities or participate in small group discussions, fearing he wouldn't measure up. This isolation only deepened his frustration, making it harder to connect with God or his church community. One day, during a quiet time of prayer, Mark came across Galatians 5:25-26: "Since we live by the Spirit, let us keep in step with the Spirit. Let us not become conceited, provoking and envying each other." These words resonated deeply with him, and he realized he had been focusing on others' spiritual paths instead of his own unique relationship with God.

Mark began to pray specifically for contentment and clarity, asking God to help him appreciate his personal spiritual journey. He also started journaling about his faith, reflecting on the small but meaningful ways he had grown over the years. Through this process, Mark saw how God had been working in his life all along—teaching him patience, humility, and perseverance. He came to understand that spiritual growth is not a competition but a personal walk with God, guided by the Spirit.

As Mark let go of comparisons, he found peace and joy in his progress. He embraced the fact that God's plan for him was unique and perfectly timed. With this newfound confidence, Mark re-engaged in his church community, using his own gifts to serve others. His journey reminded him that living by the Spirit meant focusing on God's work in his life, not on measuring up to others, and trusting that his path was exactly where God wanted him to be.

Small Prayer: Holy Spirit, guide me to walk in step with You. Help me to reject envy and embrace the unique path You have created for me. Amen.

Wednesday: Celebrating the Diversity of Gifts

Explanation of Topic: God gives diverse gifts to His children, each playing a vital role in His kingdom. Instead of envying others, we are called to celebrate and support each other's unique contributions.

Discussion Question: How does 1 Corinthians 12:4-6 encourage you to appreciate the diversity of spiritual gifts and experiences in the body of Christ? This passage teaches that "There are different kinds of gifts, but the same Spirit distributes them. There are different kinds of service, but the same Lord. There are different kinds of working, but in all of them and in everyone it is the same God at work." It emphasizes that the variety of spiritual gifts and roles within the church are all given by God for His glory and the building up of His kingdom.

Reflect on how this truth challenges you to value not only your own gifts but also the unique contributions of others. Each person has a role that is equally important to the body of Christ, whether it's teaching, encouraging, serving, or leading. By recognizing that all gifts come from the same Spirit, this passage encourages unity and gratitude rather than comparison or envy. It reminds us that God intentionally equips each believer in ways that complement one another, creating a beautifully diverse and interdependent community.

Consider how appreciating this diversity can change the way you view others in your church or spiritual community. Have you ever felt envious of someone else's gifts or dismissed the value of your own? How can this passage help you embrace your role and celebrate the unique ways God is working through others? Reflect on how focusing on the bigger picture of God's plan can inspire you to use your gifts faithfully while also encouraging and supporting those around you. How might this perspective help you foster a spirit of unity, humility, and love within the body of Christ?

Real-World Example: Rachel had been attending her church for several years and was actively involved in small group meetings and worship services. However, she often felt overlooked and insignificant compared to others who held prominent roles in the church, such as worship leaders, ministry heads, or speakers. Rachel admired their visible talents and the way they seemed to inspire others, but she couldn't shake the feeling that her own contributions were unimportant in comparison.

This sense of inadequacy began to discourage Rachel, and she started questioning her place in the church. During a Bible study, her group read 1 Corinthians 12:4-6, which emphasizes the diversity of spiritual gifts and the same Spirit working through all believers. The discussion reminded Rachel that every gift, no matter how visible or behind-the-scenes, was equally valuable in God's kingdom. Encouraged by this truth, Rachel began to pay closer attention to how God was working through her church community. She noticed the warmth and connection fostered by a member who quietly organized meals for those in need, the diligence of volunteers who kept the church running smoothly, and the heartfelt prayers of those who interceded for others.

As Rachel observed these different gifts in action, she realized that God was working through her as well, though her role might not have been as visible. She had a talent for hospitality and a knack for making newcomers feel welcome. Inspired by this realization, Rachel began focusing on her unique contributions, creating a welcoming atmosphere during church gatherings and organizing events that brought people together.

Over time, Rachel's perspective shifted. She no longer felt overlooked but empowered to serve with joy and purpose. By celebrating the gifts of others and embracing her own, Rachel found a deeper sense of belonging and fulfillment in her church community. Her experience reminded her that God's work is not confined to the spotlight but is present in every faithful act of service, no matter how small it may seem.

Small Prayer: Father, thank You for the beautiful diversity of gifts in the body of Christ. Help me to celebrate and value the ways You work in and through others. Amen.

Thursday: Practicing Empathy to Overcome Envy

Explanation of Topic: Practicing empathy—sharing in the joys and sorrows of others—helps shift our focus from comparison to community. This strengthens relationships and builds a spirit of unity and love.

Discussion Question: How can living out Romans 12:15—"Rejoice with those who rejoice; mourn with those who mourn"—help you overcome envy and foster unity? This verse invites us to actively share in the emotions and experiences of others, whether in their joys or their sorrows. By genuinely celebrating someone else's successes or comforting them in their struggles, we shift our focus from comparison to connection. This act of empathy allows us to see others through God's eyes, valuing their journey without measuring it against our own.

Rejoicing with those who rejoice can be particularly challenging when envy creeps in. It requires humility and gratitude, as well as a willingness to acknowledge that God's blessings for others do not diminish His love or plans for us. When we celebrate the achievements or spiritual growth of others, we foster a spirit of unity and love, breaking down the walls of competition and jealousy. Likewise, mourning with those who mourn reminds us that life's challenges are not meant to be faced alone. By offering support and compassion, we strengthen our bonds with others and reflect God's love in tangible ways.

Consider how practicing this verse might transform your relationships. Have there been times when envy made it difficult for you to celebrate someone else's success, or when pride kept you from empathizing with their pain? How might choosing to rejoice or mourn with others deepen your connection to them and your trust in God's timing and plans for your own life? Reflect on how living out Romans 12:15 can help you cultivate genuine relationships built on mutual encouragement, compassion, and a shared commitment to walking together in faith.

Real-World Example: Anna had been attending a Bible study group with her close friend Rachel for several months. Both had been seeking a deeper connection with God, but Anna began to notice that Rachel seemed to experience rapid spiritual growth. Rachel shared how her prayer life had deepened, how she felt closer to God than ever before, and how new opportunities for ministry were opening up for her. While Anna was happy for her friend, she couldn't ignore the pangs of envy creeping into her heart. She felt left behind, wondering why her own spiritual life felt stagnant in comparison.

At first, Anna avoided addressing her feelings, but they began to create a barrier in her friendship with Rachel. Anna found herself holding back her enthusiasm when Rachel shared her spiritual wins, and she started to feel more isolated in her own faith journey. One evening, during her quiet time, Anna read Romans 12:15: "Rejoice with those who rejoice; mourn with those who mourn." The verse convicted her. She realized that her envy was not only hurting her friendship but also preventing her from fully supporting Rachel and growing in her own walk with God.

Determined to change, Anna began to pray for her heart to be softened and for God to help her genuinely celebrate Rachel's spiritual breakthroughs. The next time Rachel shared a victory, Anna chose to rejoice with her wholeheartedly, asking questions and affirming Rachel's experiences. To her surprise, this shift not only strengthened their friendship but also inspired Anna to reexamine her own spiritual life. She realized that Rachel's growth didn't diminish her own journey but could serve as motivation for her to seek God more intentionally.

Over time, Anna's attitude changed. She no longer compared herself to Rachel but instead embraced the unique path God had for her. By rejoicing with her friend, Anna discovered a deeper connection with Rachel and found renewed energy and focus in her own spiritual walk. This experience taught her that celebrating others' successes opens the door to unity, inspiration, and a stronger sense of God's presence in all relationships.

Small Prayer: Lord, teach me to rejoice with those who rejoice and mourn with those who mourn. Help me to grow in love and empathy toward others. Amen.

Friday: Cultivating Humility

Explanation of Topic: Humility counteracts envy by encouraging us to focus on the growth and well-being of others rather than our own ambitions. It fosters a heart of service and gratitude

Discussion Question: How can Philippians 2:3-4—"Do nothing out of selfish ambition or vain conceit. Rather, in humility value others above yourselves, not looking to your own interests but each of you to the interests of the others"—guide you in practicing humility and valuing others' spiritual growth without comparison?

This passage challenges us to shift our focus from ourselves to others, fostering a mindset of humility and selflessness. Practicing humility means acknowledging that God works uniquely in every person's life, and we are not in competition with one another. By valuing others' spiritual journeys and celebrating their growth, we can build a sense of unity and encouragement within the body of Christ.

Reflect on how comparisons can create division, jealousy, or discouragement in your relationships. When you measure your spiritual progress against someone else's, you may either feel superior or inferior, neither of which aligns with God's call for humility. Philippians 2:3-4 reminds us to prioritize others' needs and celebrate their victories, knowing that their growth contributes to the greater work God is doing in His kingdom.

Consider practical ways to live out this principle. How can you intentionally encourage someone else in their faith, celebrate their milestones, or learn from their experiences? How might focusing on serving and uplifting others help you resist the temptation to compare? Reflect on how this approach fosters a spirit of gratitude and contentment, allowing you to appreciate both your own spiritual journey and the unique ways God is working in the lives of those around you. How does practicing humility draw you closer to Christ's example of selfless love and unity?

Real-World Example: James had been a faithful member of his church for many years and was widely respected for his deep knowledge of Scripture and consistent involvement in ministry. However, he occasionally found himself comparing his spiritual achievements to those of others. When he saw younger Christians stepping into leadership roles or receiving recognition, James felt a subtle sense of envy. He wondered if his contributions were being overlooked and whether his years of service still mattered in the same way.

One day, during a Bible study on Philippians 2:3-4, James felt convicted by the call to value others above himself and to prioritize their growth over his own ambitions. He realized that his focus had shifted inward, and he was missing opportunities to pour into others. James decided to make a change, choosing to intentionally support and mentor younger Christians in his church.

He began reaching out to individuals who were new to ministry, offering guidance, encouragement, and prayer. James shared his experiences, helping them navigate challenges and grow in confidence. As he invested in their journeys, he found immense joy in seeing them flourish in their faith and leadership. Instead of comparing himself to them, James celebrated their victories as if they were his own.

This shift in focus transformed James's perspective. By prioritizing the spiritual growth of others, he deepened his own faith and rediscovered the joy of selfless service. His mentorship also created a ripple effect within the church, fostering a culture of encouragement and unity. James realized that his true fulfillment came not from recognition or comparison but from reflecting Christ's love and helping others succeed in their walk with God. Through this process, he experienced the profound truth that lifting others up brings lasting joy and strengthens the entire body of Christ.

Small Prayer: Heavenly Father, help me to cultivate humility in my heart. Teach me to value and encourage others' spiritual growth, celebrating their progress without envy. Amen.

End of the Week Closing Prayer: Spiritual Envy

Heavenly Father,

We come before You with humble hearts, recognizing the moments when envy and comparison have taken root within us. Forgive us, Lord, for the times we have allowed jealousy to cloud our judgment, causing us to lose sight of the unique plans and purposes You have for our lives. Help us to remember that Your love for each of us is immeasurable and that the gifts and blessings You bestow are tailored to Your perfect design for every individual.

Teach us, Father, to genuinely celebrate the ways You are working in the lives of those around us. Let us rejoice in their victories and spiritual growth, knowing that their success reflects Your goodness and glory. Cultivate in us hearts filled with gratitude for what You have done in our own lives and humility to value others above ourselves. Help us to embrace the gifts and opportunities You have given us with contentment, trusting that they are sufficient and purposeful.

Guide us to walk in step with Your Spirit, rejecting the distractions of envy and focusing on fostering love, unity, and encouragement within the body of Christ. May we find joy in lifting up others and supporting them on their spiritual journeys. Draw us closer to You, Father, as we deepen our personal relationship with You and align our hearts with Your will.

Thank You for Your boundless grace and patience as we grow. We surrender our struggles to You, knowing that You are faithful to transform our hearts. We love You and seek to honor You in all that we do.

In Jesus' name, we pray. Amen.

Week 10: Spiritual Attachment

Introduction

Spiritual attachment refers to clinging to material possessions, relationships, or identities that hinder spiritual growth. These attachments can divert our focus from God and impede our spiritual journey. The Bible provides guidance on recognizing and overcoming such attachments to deepen our relationship with God and grow spiritually.

Definition

Spiritual Attachment: Clinging to material possessions, relationships, or identities that hinder spiritual growth.

Key Scriptures

Matthew 6:19-21 (NIV)-"Do not store up for yourselves treasures on earth, where moths and vermin destroy, and where thieves break in and steal. But store up for yourselves treasures in heaven, where moths and vermin do not destroy, and where thieves do not break in and steal. For where your treasure is, there your heart will be also."

Luke 14:26-27 (NIV)-"If anyone comes to me and does not hate father and mother, wife and children, brothers and sisters—yes, even their own life—such a person cannot be my disciple. And whoever does not carry their cross and follow me cannot be my disciple."

Philippians 3:7-8 (NIV)-"But whatever were gains to me I now consider loss for the sake of Christ. What is more, I consider everything a loss because of the surpassing worth of knowing Christ Jesus my Lord, for whose sake I have lost all things. I consider them garbage, that I may gain Christ."

1 John 2:15-17 (NIV)-"Do not love the world or anything in the world. If anyone loves the world, love for the Father is not in them. For everything in the world—the lust of the flesh, the lust of the eyes, and the pride of life—comes not from the Father but from the world. The world and its desires pass away, but whoever does the will of God lives forever."

Matthew 10:37-39 (NIV)-"Anyone who loves their father or mother more than me is not worthy of me; anyone who loves their son or daughter more than me is not worthy of me. Whoever does not take up their cross and follow me is not worthy of me. Whoever finds their life will lose it, and whoever loses their life for my sake will find it."

Monday: Prioritizing Heavenly Treasures

Explanation of Topic: This passage encourages us to prioritize eternal treasures over earthly ones. Our hearts should be focused on heavenly rewards rather than material possessions

Discussion Question: How can prioritizing heavenly treasures over earthly ones change your perspective on material possessions? Reflect on what it means to value eternal rewards—like a closer relationship with God, spiritual growth, and acts of service—above temporary, worldly gains. When you focus on heavenly treasures, your priorities shift from accumulating material wealth, status, or comfort to living in a way that reflects God's kingdom. This perspective helps you see material possessions not as ultimate goals but as tools to honor God and bless others.

Consider how this mindset can free you from the anxiety and dissatisfaction that often accompany a desire for more. Instead of viewing material possessions as a source of identity or security, trusting in heavenly treasures allows you to find true contentment in God's provision and purpose for your life. Reflect on how your approach to money, success, or possessions might change when you focus on eternal values. How can this perspective help you live with generosity, gratitude, and faith, knowing that your ultimate treasure is with God?

Real-World Example: Alex had always believed that success was defined by wealth and material achievements. He worked tirelessly to climb the corporate ladder, dedicating long hours to his job and making significant sacrifices in his personal life. Over time, Alex amassed the possessions he had dreamed of—a large home, a luxury car, and financial security. Yet, despite these accomplishments, he felt an unshakable sense of emptiness and dissatisfaction. The joy he thought material wealth would bring never arrived, and he felt burdened by the constant pressure to maintain his lifestyle.

One day, during a sermon at church, Alex heard Matthew 6:19-21: "Do not store up for yourselves treasures on earth, where moths and vermin destroy, and where thieves break in and steal. But store up for yourselves treasures in heaven." The message struck a deep chord in his heart. Alex realized that he had been chasing temporary possessions while neglecting the eternal values of spiritual growth, relationships, and serving others.

Determined to shift his focus, Alex began to prioritize time with God through prayer, studying Scripture, and joining a small group at his church. He also started volunteering at a local shelter, using his resources to bless others rather than striving for more material gain. As Alex invested in his spiritual life and relationships, he began to experience a profound sense of peace and fulfillment. His perspective on wealth and possessions changed—no longer were they a source of identity or worth, but tools to reflect God's love and generosity. By focusing on eternal values, Alex found joy and contentment that no material possession could ever provide.

Small Prayer: Lord, help me to focus on storing up treasures in heaven. Reveal to me any attachments that hinder my spiritual growth, and help me to prioritize my relationship with You. Amen.

Tuesday: Putting Jesus First

Explanation of Topic: Jesus emphasizes the need to prioritize our relationship with Him above all else, including family and personal relationships. True discipleship requires putting Jesus first.

Discussion Question: In what ways does Luke 14:26-27 challenge you to put Jesus first in your relationships and personal life? This passage, where Jesus says, "If anyone comes to me and does not hate father and mother, wife and children, brothers and sisters—yes, even their own life—such a person cannot be my disciple. And whoever does not carry their cross and follow me cannot be my disciple," may seem harsh at first glance. However, it emphasizes the level of devotion Jesus requires, where our love for Him must surpass all other attachments.

Reflect on how this teaching challenges you to examine the priorities in your life. Are there relationships, goals, or personal desires that sometimes take precedence over your commitment to Christ? Putting Jesus first doesn't mean neglecting or disregarding others, but it does mean ensuring that your relationship with Him shapes and informs all other aspects of your life. It calls for a willingness to surrender anything that might hinder your walk with Him, even if it's something as deeply ingrained as familial bonds or personal ambitions.

Consider the areas of your life where you might struggle to fully submit to Christ's lordship. How might prioritizing Jesus above all else transform your relationships, career, or daily decisions? What practical steps can you take to carry your cross daily, sacrificing comfort or convenience to follow Him wholeheartedly? This passage invites you to live with a heart that places Jesus at the center, trusting that He will guide and bless all other areas of your life when you seek Him first

Real-World Example: Maria, a dedicated wife and mother, had always placed a high value on her family. She spent her days juggling work, household responsibilities, and the needs of her children and husband. While Maria loved her family deeply, the constant demands left little time for her personal relationship with God. Over time, she noticed that her faith was taking a backseat—prayer became rushed, Bible study was sporadic, and her church involvement began to dwindle. She felt torn, wanting to grow spiritually but also fearing that prioritizing her faith might cause her to neglect her family's needs.

One Sunday, Maria heard a sermon on Luke 14:26-27, where Jesus calls His disciples to put Him above all else, even family. At first, the idea felt daunting and guilt-inducing. How could she prioritize Jesus when her family needed so much of her? But as she reflected further, Maria realized that putting Christ first didn't mean abandoning her family; it meant allowing her relationship with Him to guide and shape her role as a wife and mother. She saw that by prioritizing time with Jesus, she could better serve and love her family with patience, wisdom, and grace.

Maria began waking up earlier to spend quiet moments in prayer and Scripture before the day's demands set in. She also involved her family in her spiritual journey, encouraging them to pray together and attend church as a unit. This shift brought unexpected blessings. Maria found herself more equipped to handle stress and more present in her interactions with her family. Her relationship with Christ became the anchor that strengthened her family life, and she realized that putting Him first allowed her to fulfill her responsibilities with a renewed sense of purpose and peace.

By balancing her devotion to Christ with her family commitments, Maria discovered that prioritizing her faith wasn't a burden but a source of strength that enriched every aspect of her life.

Small Prayer: Jesus, help me to put You first in all areas of my life. Give me the strength to prioritize my relationship with You above all else. Amen.

Wednesday: Valuing Christ Above Worldly Gains

Explanation of Topic: Paul demonstrates the attitude of valuing Christ above all worldly gains. Everything else is insignificant compared to the worth of knowing Jesus.

Discussion Question: How does Philippians 3:7-8 inspire you to value your relationship with Christ above all worldly gains? In this passage, Paul writes, "But whatever were gains to me I now consider loss for the sake of Christ. What is more, I consider everything a loss because of the surpassing worth of knowing Christ Jesus my Lord, for whose sake I have lost all things. I consider them garbage, that I may gain Christ." These verses reflect Paul's radical shift in priorities. Once proud of his accomplishments, status, and religious achievements, Paul came to see them as worthless compared to the immeasurable value of knowing Christ.

Reflect on what this means in your own life. Are there worldly gains—such as success, possessions, recognition, or even personal ambitions—that you may hold onto too tightly? How might valuing Christ above these things transform your perspective? Paul's words challenge us to assess what we are pursuing and to ask ourselves if those pursuits bring us closer to Christ or distract us from Him.

Consider how prioritizing your relationship with Jesus might change the way you view your goals and possessions. Would you be willing to let go of something significant if it stood in the way of deepening your walk with Him? Reflect on how knowing Christ gives a sense of eternal purpose, peace, and fulfillment that no worldly gain can match. How can you take steps today to align your heart and actions with the eternal treasure of knowing Christ above all else?

Real-World Example: James was a highly successful professional, celebrated in his field for his achievements and dedication. He had worked tirelessly to earn promotions, accolades, and financial security, believing these accomplishments would bring him happiness and fulfillment. From the outside, James seemed to have it all—a prestigious career, a luxurious home, and the admiration of his peers. Yet, despite his success, James often felt a deep sense of emptiness. The joy he expected from his achievements never seemed to last, and the pressure to maintain his status left him constantly striving but never satisfied.

One Sunday, James attended a church service where the pastor preached on Philippians 3:7-8. Paul's words about considering all worldly gains as loss compared to knowing Christ struck a chord in James's heart. He realized that while he had built his life around professional success, his relationship with Christ had been neglected. His accomplishments had become his identity, leaving little room for the eternal purpose and joy that only Christ could provide.

This realization led James to reevaluate his priorities. He began spending time in prayer and Scripture each morning, seeking to rebuild his relationship with God. As he did, he found a sense of peace and fulfillment that no promotion or paycheck had ever brought him. James also started using his resources and skills to serve others, mentoring younger professionals and supporting community outreach programs through his church.

Over time, James came to see his achievements not as ends in themselves but as tools to glorify God and bless others. He still worked diligently, but his motivation shifted from personal gain to honoring Christ in all he did. The joy and fulfillment he once sought in worldly success were now rooted in his deepening relationship with Jesus. For James, knowing Christ became the ultimate treasure, far surpassing any status or accomplishment the world could offer.

Small Prayer: Father, help me to see the surpassing worth of knowing Christ. May I consider all else as loss in comparison to Him. Amen.

Thursday: Rejecting Love for the World

Explanation of Topic: Loving the world and its desires is incompatible with loving God. This passage calls us to focus on doing God's will, which leads to eternal life.

Discussion Question: How does 1 John 2:15-17 warn against the dangers of loving the world? In this passage, John writes, "Do not love the world or anything in the world. If anyone loves the world, love for the Father is not in them. For everything in the world—the lust of the flesh, the lust of the eyes, and the pride of life—comes not from the Father but from the world. The world and its desires pass away, but whoever does the will of God lives forever." These verses caution us against becoming attached to the fleeting pleasures, possessions, and ambitions that the world offers. Such desires often lead to spiritual distraction and pull our hearts away from a deeper relationship with God.

Reflect on how the "lust of the flesh" (pursuit of physical gratification), the "lust of the eyes" (envy and materialism), and the "pride of life" (arrogance and self-reliance) may tempt you to prioritize worldly things over your spiritual life. How have these distractions impacted your focus on God's will and eternal values? John's reminder that these desires are temporary emphasizes the need to align our lives with God's purposes, which bring eternal rewards.

Consider steps you can take to focus on doing God's will. This might include reevaluating how you spend your time and resources, intentionally seeking God through prayer and Scripture, or choosing to serve others rather than pursuing self-centered goals. Reflect on how shifting your focus from worldly desires to God's will can deepen your faith, bring lasting fulfillment, and draw you closer to the eternal life promised to those who follow Him. How might letting go of worldly attachments free you to live fully in God's purpose for your life?

Real-World Example: Rachel was a young professional living in a fast-paced city, constantly surrounded by societal pressures to achieve success, accumulate wealth, and maintain a glamorous lifestyle. Social media amplified these pressures, as she often compared herself to friends and influencers who seemed to have it all—luxury vacations, expensive possessions, and picture-perfect lives. Rachel worked long hours at her job, driven by a desire to prove her worth and keep up with the expectations of those around her. Yet, despite her efforts, she felt increasingly overwhelmed, restless, and unfulfilled.

One evening, during a church Bible study, the group read 1 John 2:15-17. The passage about the dangers of loving the world struck Rachel deeply. She realized that her pursuit of worldly desires—the approval of others, material success, and social status—had left her spiritually empty. She had been so focused on these fleeting goals that she had neglected her relationship with God and lost sight of her true purpose.

Determined to make a change, Rachel began to reevaluate her priorities. She spent time in prayer, asking God to help her release her attachment to worldly desires and refocus her heart on Him. She set boundaries at work, allowing more time for rest, worship, and serving in her church community. Rachel also reduced her time on social media, which had fueled her envy and discontent, and instead spent time meditating on Scriptures that reminded her of her worth in Christ and the eternal rewards of following Him.

As Rachel pursued God's will over societal expectations, she experienced a profound sense of clarity and peace. No longer striving for validation from the world, she found joy in living with a purpose rooted in her faith. By aligning her life with God's will, Rachel discovered the freedom to focus on what truly mattered—building her relationship with God and using her talents to bless others.

Small Prayer: Lord, help me to reject the love of the world and its desires. Teach me to focus on doing Your will and seeking eternal life in You. Amen.

Friday: Prioritizing Love for Jesus

Explanation of Topic: True discipleship involves prioritizing our love for Jesus above all other relationships and attachments. This commitment may involve sacrifice, but it leads to true life.

Discussion Question: How does Matthew 10:37-39 emphasize the importance of prioritizing your love for Jesus above all other attachments? In this passage, Jesus says, "Anyone who loves their father or mother more than me is not worthy of me; anyone who loves their son or daughter more than me is not worthy of me. Whoever does not take up their cross and follow me is not worthy of me. Whoever finds their life will lose it, and whoever loses their life for my sake will find it." These verses challenge us to examine the depth of our commitment to Christ and the place He holds in our hearts compared to the people and things we cherish most.

This teaching highlights that our relationship with Jesus must take precedence over all other relationships and attachments, even those closest to us. It does not mean abandoning or disregarding our loved ones but ensuring that our devotion to Christ shapes and guides those relationships. Loving Jesus above all else allows us to love others with a purer, more selfless love rooted in Him.

Reflect on the metaphor of taking up your cross. How does this symbolize a willingness to sacrifice comfort, personal ambitions, or even the approval of others to follow Jesus? Consider areas in your life where attachments—whether to relationships, career goals, or personal desires—might sometimes compete with your devotion to Christ. What practical steps can you take to ensure that He remains your highest priority? How might fully surrendering these attachments bring a deeper sense of purpose and fulfillment in your walk with Him? This passage invites you to find your true life by losing it for Christ's sake, trusting that He will guide you to what is eternally meaningful and rewarding.

Real-World Example: Karen was a devoted wife and mother who deeply loved her family and dedicated much of her time to their well-being. She managed the household, supported her children's activities, and prioritized family traditions, often sacrificing her own needs to ensure that her family felt cared for and supported. However, as life became busier, Karen noticed her personal relationship with Christ taking a backseat. Prayer and Bible study were rushed or skipped entirely, and her time with church became sporadic. While she cherished her family, she felt a growing sense of spiritual emptiness and disconnection from God.

One Sunday, Karen heard a sermon on Matthew 10:37-39, where Jesus calls His followers to prioritize their love for Him above all other attachments, even family. The message convicted her. She realized that while she was serving her family well, she was not placing Jesus at the center of her life. Her devotion to her family, while good, had unintentionally overshadowed her devotion to Christ. She understood that by prioritizing her love for Jesus, she could better love and lead her family in faith.

Determined to make a change, Karen began intentionally carving out time for her personal relationship with God. She committed to starting each day with prayer and Scripture reading, asking God to guide her as a wife and mother. She also began encouraging her family to join her in faith-building activities, such as attending church together and sharing devotionals as a family.

As Karen placed Christ first, she noticed a significant shift in her life. Her spiritual fulfillment deepened, and she felt more patient, compassionate, and centered in her interactions with her family. Her decision to prioritize Jesus not only strengthened her faith but also enriched her relationships, as her family saw the peace and joy that came from her renewed devotion. Karen learned that loving Christ above all else didn't detract from her family life—it enhanced it, allowing her to love them more fully and lead them closer to Him.

Small Prayer: Jesus, help me to love You above all else. Give me the courage to take up my cross and follow You wholeheartedly. Amen.

End of the Week Closing Prayer for Spiritual Attachment

Heavenly Father,

We come before You, recognizing how easily we cling to material possessions, relationships, and worldly identities that can hinder our spiritual growth and draw us away from You. Forgive us for the times we have placed these things above our love and devotion to You. Lord, we ask for Your wisdom to discern what truly matters and for the strength to release the attachments that weigh us down.

Help us to store up treasures in heaven, valuing the eternal over the temporary, and to follow Jesus with wholehearted devotion. Teach us to find our worth, identity, and fulfillment in Christ alone, knowing that nothing in this world compares to the joy of knowing and serving You. Transform our hearts to seek You first, trusting that everything else will fall into place according to Your perfect will.

In Jesus' name, we pray. Amen.

Week 11: Spiritual Apathy

Introduction

Spiritual apathy is characterized by indifference or a lack of interest in spiritual matters. This condition can lead to stagnation in one's faith journey and a disconnection from God. The Bible provides guidance on rekindling passion for spiritual growth and maintaining a vibrant relationship with God.

Definition

Spiritual Apathy: Indifference or lack of interest in spiritual matters.

Key Scriptures

Revelation 3:15-16 (NIV)-"I know your deeds, that you are neither cold nor hot. I wish you were either one or the other! So, because you are lukewarm—neither hot nor cold—I am about to spit you out of my mouth."

Romans 12:11 (NIV)-"Never be lacking in zeal, but keep your spiritual fervor, serving the Lord."

Hebrews 6:11-12 (NIV)-"We want each of you to show this same diligence to the very end, so that what you hope for may be fully realized. We do not want you to become lazy, but to imitate those who through faith and patience inherit what has been promised."

Matthew 5:6 (NIV)-"Blessed are those who hunger and thirst for righteousness, for they will be filled."

Colossians 3:23-24 (NIV)-"Whatever you do, work at it with all your heart, as working for the Lord, not for human masters, since you know that you will receive an inheritance from the Lord as a reward. It is the Lord Christ you are serving."

Monday: Lukewarm Faith

Explanation of Topic: This passage addresses the dangers of lukewarm faith and calls for fervency in our relationship with God. Spiritual apathy displeases God and hinders our spiritual effectiveness.

Discussion Question: How does being lukewarm in your faith affect your relationship with God and your spiritual impact? Revelation 3:16 warns against lukewarm faith, where Jesus says, "So, because you are lukewarm—neither hot nor cold—I am about to spit you out of my mouth." Lukewarm faith is characterized by complacency, a lack of passion for God, and a tendency to go through the motions of religion without genuine connection or commitment. This spiritual indifference not only weakens your relationship with God but also diminishes your ability to influence others positively for His kingdom.

When your faith is lukewarm, it becomes harder to hear God's voice and sense His guidance. Prayer and Scripture reading may feel like empty routines rather than vibrant connections with the Creator. This lack of intimacy with God can lead to a sense of spiritual stagnation, where growth is stunted, and the joy and peace found in Christ are replaced by apathy or distraction.

Lukewarm faith also impacts your spiritual witness. Without a wholehearted commitment to Christ, it becomes difficult to inspire or encourage others in their faith. A life that appears indifferent to God's transformative power can create confusion or even discouragement for those looking to see Christ reflected in you.

Reflect on areas of your life where your faith might feel lukewarm. Are there practices or attitudes that have become routine or lack passion? How has this affected your ability to connect deeply with God and share His love with others? Consider practical steps to rekindle your faith, such as setting aside intentional time for prayer, diving deeper into God's Word, or engaging in community worship. How might living with renewed fervor and commitment transform both your relationship with God and the spiritual impact you have on those around you?

Real-World Example: Megan had once been deeply passionate about her faith. She eagerly attended church services, led Bible studies, and spent hours in prayer and Scripture reading. Her relationship with God felt alive and vibrant, and her enthusiasm inspired those around her. However, over time, life's demands began to chip away at her spiritual habits. Work became more demanding, family obligations grew heavier, and Megan started prioritizing other activities over her time with God.

At first, she didn't notice the change. Missing a day of prayer or skipping a church service felt harmless. But soon, those days turned into weeks, and Megan found herself going through the motions of her faith without the deep connection she once felt. She still attended church and volunteered occasionally, but her heart wasn't fully in it. The passion she once had was replaced by a sense of indifference, and her spiritual life felt stagnant and dry.

This lukewarm approach began to affect other areas of her life. Megan felt increasingly disconnected from her purpose, struggling to find joy or fulfillment in her daily activities. Her indifference toward her faith made it harder to encourage or uplift others, and she began to feel isolated, even within her church community. Megan missed the closeness she once had with God but felt unsure how to reignite her passion.

One evening, she read Revelation 3:15-16, where Jesus speaks against being lukewarm. The words hit her deeply, and Megan realized she had allowed complacency to take over her faith. Determined to change, she started setting aside intentional time each morning to pray and read Scripture, even if it meant waking up earlier. She also joined a small group to reconnect with her community and find accountability. Slowly, as she prioritized her relationship with God, Megan began to feel her passion returning. The spiritual dryness lifted, replaced by a renewed sense of purpose and joy in serving God.

Megan's journey reminded her that faith requires intentionality and devotion. By rekindling her passion, she not only restored her relationship with God but also rediscovered the joy of inspiring and encouraging others in their spiritual walk.

Small Prayer: Lord, reignite my passion for You. Help me to recognize areas of my life where apathy has taken hold and guide me towards renewal. Amen.

Tuesday: Maintaining Zeal

Explanation of Topic: Paul encourages believers to maintain their enthusiasm and dedication in serving the Lord. This verse underscores the importance of sustaining passion and commitment in our spiritual lives

Discussion Question: In what ways does Romans 12:11—"Never be lacking in zeal, but keep your spiritual fervor, serving the Lord"— encourage you to maintain zeal and fervor in your spiritual life? This verse calls believers to be passionate and committed in their faith, urging them not to allow complacency, distractions, or weariness to diminish their devotion to God. Maintaining zeal means having an eager desire to serve the Lord and pursuing Him with enthusiasm and purpose, even in the face of challenges.

Reflect on how a lack of zeal can lead to spiritual stagnation, where worship feels routine, prayer becomes infrequent, and acts of service lose their joy. Romans 12:11 reminds us that a fervent spirit is essential for staying connected to God and fulfilling His calling in our lives. This kind of zeal is not based on fleeting emotions but is rooted in a deep love for God and a desire to bring Him glory.

Consider practical ways to nurture spiritual fervor in your life. Are there areas where you've become distracted, discouraged, or overwhelmed? How can you rekindle your passion for God and His work? This might involve renewing your prayer life, surrounding yourself with other passionate believers, or reflecting on the ways God has been faithful in the past. Serving others is another powerful way to reignite zeal, as it shifts your focus from yourself to God's mission.

Think about how maintaining zeal impacts your relationship with God and your witness to others. A life filled with spiritual fervor inspires those around you, demonstrating the transformative power of a vibrant faith. How can you apply the encouragement in this verse to overcome spiritual fatigue or apathy and pursue God's work with renewed enthusiasm?

Reflect on how committing to fervent service for the Lord can deepen your joy and strengthen your connection with Him.

Real-World Example: Jason is a long-time member of his church who actively serves in multiple ministries. Over the years, he has volunteered as a youth group leader, participated in mission trips, and helped with community outreach events. While many others have experienced burnout or spiritual fatigue, Jason has managed to remain spiritually vibrant and deeply connected to God. His secret lies in the way he approaches his service—not as an obligation, but as an expression of his love for God and others.

Every morning, Jason begins his day with intentional prayer, asking God for guidance, strength, and a heart ready to serve. He meditates on verses like Romans 12:11: "Never be lacking in zeal, but keep your spiritual fervor, serving the Lord." This Scripture serves as a reminder that his energy and enthusiasm for ministry come not from his own strength but from the Spirit working within him.

Jason also finds joy in the relationships he builds through service. Whether mentoring teenagers, organizing food drives, or simply encouraging a fellow volunteer, he sees each interaction as an opportunity to reflect Christ's love. When challenges arise—such as difficult schedules or unexpected setbacks—Jason remains steadfast by focusing on the eternal impact of his work. He views every effort as a way to glorify God and fulfill his role in God's kingdom.

To stay spiritually vibrant, Jason prioritizes rest and personal growth. He takes time to recharge by attending retreats, studying Scripture deeply, and surrounding himself with supportive believers who encourage his faith journey. By maintaining a balance between serving others and nurturing his own relationship with God, Jason avoids the pitfalls of burnout and apathy.

His consistent zeal not only fuels his own spiritual life but also inspires those around him. People in his church and community often remark on his contagious joy and unwavering dedication. Jason's life is a testament to how serving with humility, passion, and a focus on God's glory can lead to a deeply fulfilling and spiritually vibrant life.

Small Prayer: Father, fill me with zeal and fervor for Your work. Inspire me daily to serve You with enthusiasm and dedication. Amen.

Wednesday: Diligence in Faith

Explanation of Topic: The writer of Hebrews urges diligence and warns against laziness in the spiritual journey. Consistent effort and perseverance are essential for realizing God's promises

Discussion Question: How does Hebrews 6:11-12—"We want each of you to show this same diligence to the very end, so that what you hope for may be fully realized. We do not want you to become lazy, but to imitate those who through faith and patience inherit what has been promised"—challenge you to be diligent and avoid spiritual laziness?

This passage calls believers to maintain a consistent and active faith, urging them not to become complacent or sluggish in their spiritual pursuits. Spiritual laziness often manifests as neglecting prayer, Scripture reading, worship, or service, leading to stagnation in one's relationship with God. Instead, the writer of Hebrews encourages diligence—an intentional and persistent effort to grow in faith and remain steadfast in hope.

Reflect on what diligence in your spiritual life might look like. Are there areas where you have become inconsistent or passive, perhaps prioritizing other responsibilities or distractions over your time with God? This passage reminds us that spiritual growth requires intentionality and patience, as it often involves persevering through seasons of waiting or challenge.

The verse also points to the importance of imitating faithful examples. Consider how observing the lives of spiritually mature believers—those who demonstrate unwavering faith and endurance—can inspire and motivate you. Their commitment to following God, even in difficult circumstances, serves as a model for how to pursue a vibrant and active faith.

What steps can you take to cultivate diligence in your spiritual walk? This might involve setting aside dedicated time for prayer and Bible study, engaging in acts of service, or joining a small group for accountability and encouragement. Reflect on how these actions can help you stay focused on God's promises and deepen your trust in His plan. How might this diligence not only strengthen your personal faith but also equip you to encourage others in their spiritual journeys?

Real-World Example: Sarah, a dedicated Christian, made a decision early in her faith journey to prioritize her spiritual growth by actively engaging with her church community. She regularly attended Bible studies and joined a weekly prayer group, seeing these as opportunities to deepen her understanding of God's Word and build meaningful relationships with other believers. While her schedule was busy with work and family responsibilities, Sarah intentionally carved out time for these gatherings, recognizing their importance in nurturing her faith.

Through the Bible studies, Sarah gained a richer perspective on Scripture, often uncovering insights she might have missed on her own. The discussions challenged her to apply biblical truths to her daily life and strengthened her confidence in sharing her faith. The prayer group became a source of encouragement and accountability. Whether celebrating answered prayers or supporting one another through difficult seasons, Sarah found that the collective faith of the group inspired her to stay steadfast in her own walk with God.

Sarah's consistent participation also helped her develop spiritual discipline outside of these gatherings. She began setting aside quiet time each day for personal prayer and reflection, building on what she learned in her community settings. Over time, Sarah noticed significant spiritual growth—her patience deepened, her trust in God strengthened, and her ability to handle life's challenges with grace improved.

Her commitment not only enriched her own faith but also positively impacted those around her. Sarah became a source of wisdom and encouragement in her church, often mentoring newer believers and sharing how the combination of Bible study, prayer, and community had transformed her life. By staying diligent and engaged in these spiritual practices, Sarah found consistent growth and the encouragement needed to persevere in her faith journey, serving as an example of the benefits of an active, intentional commitment to God.

Small Prayer: Lord, help me to be diligent in my faith. Give me the perseverance to continue seeking You, even when I feel weary. Amen.

Thursday: Hunger for Righteousness

Explanation of Topic: Jesus promises fulfillment to those who earnestly seek righteousness. A deep longing for spiritual growth and righteousness counters apathy and leads to satisfaction in God.

Discussion Question: How does Matthew 5:6—"Blessed are those who hunger and thirst for righteousness, for they will be filled"—inspire you to cultivate a hunger and thirst for righteousness? This verse highlights the deep, passionate desire to live in alignment with God's will and to pursue a life marked by holiness, justice, and love. Jesus promises that those who earnestly seek righteousness will be satisfied, not with temporary or worldly rewards, but with the fullness of God's presence and His transformative work in their lives.

Reflect on the imagery of hunger and thirst. Just as physical hunger and thirst drive us to seek nourishment, spiritual hunger should prompt us to actively pursue God through prayer, Scripture, worship, and acts of obedience. This kind of longing requires humility, acknowledging that only God can truly satisfy the deepest needs of our soul.

Consider how cultivating a hunger for righteousness shapes your priorities and actions. Are there distractions or habits in your life that dull your appetite for spiritual growth? What changes can you make to deepen your longing for God? This might involve creating a dedicated time for prayer, committing to study the Bible more intentionally, or surrounding yourself with a community of believers who inspire and challenge you to grow.

Reflect also on how a hunger for righteousness influences your relationships with others. Pursuing righteousness isn't just about personal growth; it includes seeking justice, showing mercy, and reflecting God's character in your interactions. How can your desire for spiritual growth lead you to make a positive impact in the lives of those around you?

Lastly, think about the promise in this verse—that God will fill those who seek Him. How does this assurance encourage you to persevere, even when spiritual growth feels slow or challenging? What practical steps can you take today to nurture your hunger and thirst for righteousness and draw closer to the One who satisfies?

Real-World Example: Michael, a young professional, felt a deep desire to grow closer to God and live out his faith more intentionally. He realized that his spiritual life had become routine, and he longed for a renewed sense of purpose and connection with God. Inspired by Matthew 5:6, which promises that those who hunger and thirst for righteousness will be filled, Michael committed himself to cultivating a more vibrant faith.

He began by incorporating personal spiritual disciplines into his daily life. Each morning, Michael spent time in prayer and Scripture meditation, seeking God's guidance and reflecting on how to align his life more closely with His will. Once a month, Michael practiced fasting—not just abstaining from food, but also dedicating the time he would have spent eating to prayer and worship. Through these practices, he felt a deeper sense of dependence on God and clarity about His purpose for his life.

Michael didn't stop at personal disciplines; he also sought communal spiritual growth. He joined a small group at his church, where members encouraged one another to live out their faith authentically. Together, they studied the Bible, prayed for each other, and discussed practical ways to apply biblical principles in their daily lives. This sense of community deepened Michael's understanding of righteousness as not just personal holiness but also loving and serving others.

Driven by his desire to reflect God's justice and mercy, Michael began volunteering at a local shelter. Acts of service became a tangible way for him to live out his faith, showing God's love to those in need. Through these interactions, he experienced the joy and fulfillment that comes from aligning his actions with God's heart for compassion and justice.

Over time, Michael noticed profound changes in his spiritual life. The practices of prayer, fasting, and service strengthened his relationship with God and gave him a sense of peace and purpose he had never felt before. His commitment to seeking righteousness not only transformed his own life but also inspired those around him to pursue a deeper connection with God. Michael's journey demonstrated that actively hungering and thirsting for righteousness leads to a life filled with God's presence, joy, and satisfaction.

Small Prayer: Jesus, create in me a hunger and thirst for righteousness. Guide me to take steps that deepen my spiritual growth. Amen.

Friday: Wholehearted Service

Explanation of Topic: Serving the Lord wholeheartedly in all we do fosters a sense of purpose and dedication. This perspective helps combat spiritual apathy by aligning our daily actions with our spiritual calling.

Discussion Question: How can Colossians 3:23-24—"Whatever you do, work at it with all your heart, as working for the Lord, not for human masters, since you know that you will receive an inheritance from the Lord as a reward. It is the Lord Christ you are serving"—help you find motivation and purpose in serving the Lord wholeheartedly in all aspects of your life?

This passage reframes how we approach our daily tasks, responsibilities, and roles, whether they seem significant or mundane. It reminds us that everything we do—at work, at home, in ministry, or in relationships—is an opportunity to serve God and bring Him glory. By shifting our perspective from pleasing others or meeting worldly expectations to honoring the Lord, we can find deeper purpose and motivation, even in the most routine activities.

Reflect on areas of your life where you may struggle with motivation or feel disconnected from God's purpose. How does viewing these responsibilities as acts of service to the Lord change your attitude? For example, caring for your family, completing work tasks, or volunteering becomes more meaningful when done with the mindset that you're serving Christ Himself. This perspective encourages excellence, perseverance, and joy, as your efforts are not tied to human recognition but to an eternal inheritance promised by God.

Consider how this mindset impacts your character and spiritual growth. Working wholeheartedly for the Lord fosters discipline, humility, and gratitude, reminding you that God sees and values your efforts, even when others may not. It also encourages you to serve with integrity and love, reflecting Christ's character in all you do.

What practical steps can you take to align your daily actions with this principle? This might involve starting your day by dedicating your tasks to God, asking Him for guidance and strength, or finding moments throughout the day to pause and reflect on how your actions can glorify Him. How might embracing this perspective bring renewed energy and purpose to every area of your life, helping you find joy in serving the Lord wholeheartedly?

Real-World Example: Karen worked as a school teacher in a small community, a job she loved but often found exhausting. Between long hours of lesson planning, managing a classroom of energetic children, and meeting the expectations of parents and administrators, she sometimes questioned whether her work truly made a difference. It was easy to get caught up in the routine and feel as though her efforts were unnoticed or undervalued.

One Sunday, during a sermon on Colossians 3:23-24, Karen's perspective shifted. The pastor explained how viewing work as an act of service to the Lord could transform even the most ordinary tasks into acts of worship. The verse challenged Karen to approach her teaching with a renewed sense of purpose, reminding her that her ultimate "boss" wasn't her school administration but the Lord Himself.

Karen began to pray each morning before stepping into her classroom, asking God to help her teach with patience, wisdom, and love. She also started looking at her students not just as learners but as individuals with unique needs, dreams, and struggles. Viewing her job as a mission field, she found new opportunities to reflect Christ's love—by encouraging a struggling student, listening to a parent's concerns with compassion, or supporting a colleague going through a tough time.

This mindset gave Karen a sense of joy and fulfillment she hadn't experienced before. Instead of focusing on the challenges or seeking recognition, she poured herself into her work with integrity and dedication, knowing she was serving God through her actions. Her attitude didn't go unnoticed. Parents appreciated her genuine care for their children, and her colleagues admired her positivity and perseverance.

Over time, Karen realized that her work wasn't just about teaching academics—it was about showing God's love through her words and actions. By approaching her job as a way to serve the Lord, Karen found deeper motivation and purpose in her everyday tasks. This shift not only enriched her own spiritual life but also made her a source of encouragement and inspiration to those around her.

Small Prayer: Lord, help me to serve You wholeheartedly in all I do. Let my actions reflect my love and dedication to You. Amen.

End of the Week Closing Prayer for Spiritual Apathy

Heavenly Father,

We humbly come before You, acknowledging the times when spiritual apathy has crept into our hearts. We confess the moments when we have become indifferent, distracted, or weary, neglecting the passion and devotion You deserve. Forgive us, Lord, for allowing our love for You to grow cold and for prioritizing worldly concerns over our relationship with You.

Father, we ask for Your guidance and renewal. Rekindle within us a deep hunger and thirst for righteousness, a desire to know You more intimately, and a passion to live out Your will in every aspect of our lives. Remind us of the joy and fulfillment that come from seeking You wholeheartedly and help us to turn back to You with fresh zeal and purpose.

Renew our minds and hearts, Lord, so that we may serve You with all our strength, giving You the best of our time, talents, and efforts. Surround us with a supportive community of believers who will encourage, challenge, and hold us accountable as we grow closer to You. Teach us to lean on Your Spirit for strength and guidance, knowing that apart from You, we can do nothing.

Thank You, Father, for Your endless grace and patience as we navigate our spiritual journeys. Thank You for never giving up on us, even when we fall short. May our lives reflect Your glory, and may our renewed passion inspire others to draw near to You.

In Jesus' name, we pray. Amen.

Week 12: Spiritual Doubt

Introduction

Spiritual doubt is the feeling of uncertainty or skepticism about one's faith, beliefs, or spiritual experiences. This condition can lead to confusion, fear, and a weakened relationship with God. However, the Bible provides encouragement and assurance for those struggling with doubt, guiding them toward a deeper and more resilient faith.

Definition

Spiritual Doubt: Uncertainty or skepticism about one's faith, beliefs, or spiritual experiences.

Key Scriptures

James 1:5-6 (NIV)-"If any of you lacks wisdom, you should ask God, who gives generously to all without finding fault, and it will be given to you. But when you ask, you must believe and not doubt, because the one who doubts is like a wave of the sea, blown and tossed by the wind."

Mark 9:24 (NIV)-"Immediately the boy's father exclaimed, 'I do believe; help me overcome my unbelief!'"

Matthew 14:31 (NIV)-"Immediately Jesus reached out his hand and caught him. 'You of little faith,' he said, 'why did you doubt?'"

Hebrews 11:1 (NIV)-"Now faith is confidence in what we hope for and assurance about what we do not see."

Psalm 94:19 (NIV)-"When anxiety was great within me, your consolation brought me joy."

Monday: Seeking Wisdom

Explanation of Topic: This passage encourages seeking God's wisdom and underscores the importance of faith without doubt. Trusting in God's generosity and guidance can help stabilize our faith.

Discussion Question: How does seeking wisdom from God help in overcoming doubt? Doubt often arises when we face uncertainty, unanswered questions, or situations that seem beyond our understanding. Left unchecked, it can shake our faith and create a sense of spiritual instability. However, James 1:5 offers reassurance, stating, "If any of you lacks wisdom, you should ask God, who gives generously to all without finding fault, and it will be given to you." Seeking wisdom from God allows us to move beyond our limited perspective and gain clarity through His infinite understanding.

Godly wisdom helps us view our doubts not as obstacles but as opportunities to grow in faith. Instead of relying solely on human reasoning, seeking wisdom through prayer and Scripture invites God to illuminate His truth, offering guidance and reassurance. This wisdom doesn't always provide immediate answers to all our questions but grants us the peace to trust God's timing and sovereignty, even in uncertainty.

Reflect on how God's wisdom can shift your perspective. Have you experienced moments of doubt where asking for His guidance brought clarity or comfort? How did it change your response to the situation? Seeking wisdom also strengthens your faith by deepening your relationship with God, reminding you that He is a trustworthy source of truth and direction.

Consider practical steps you can take to seek God's wisdom when faced with doubt. This might include spending time in prayer, meditating on Scripture, seeking counsel from spiritually mature believers, or journaling to process your thoughts and hear God's voice more clearly. How might this intentional pursuit of God's wisdom equip you to overcome doubt and live with greater confidence in His plan for your life? Reflect on how God's wisdom not only addresses your doubts but also strengthens your ability to trust Him fully, even when the path ahead is unclear.

Real-World Example: Sarah was at a crossroads in her life, faced with a major decision about whether to accept a new job opportunity in a different city. On the surface, the offer seemed promising—a higher salary, better career prospects, and the chance to live in a vibrant new environment. However, the move would mean leaving her close-knit church community, her family, and the ministry work she had been deeply involved in for years. The conflicting emotions left Sarah feeling anxious and uncertain. She doubted her ability to make the right choice and feared stepping out of God's will.

Recognizing her need for guidance, Sarah turned to James 1:5, which promises that God generously gives wisdom to those who ask. She began to pray daily, asking God for clarity and peace about her decision. Rather than rushing into a choice, Sarah committed to waiting on God's direction. During her prayer times, she journaled her thoughts, wrote down Scriptures that spoke to her, and listened for God's voice.

As she sought wisdom, Sarah also sought counsel from trusted mentors in her church. They reminded her to consider not only the practical benefits of the job but also how it aligned with God's purpose for her life. Through their guidance, she realized that while the job offered great potential, it might not allow her the time or opportunities to continue serving in ministry, which was deeply important to her.

Over time, Sarah felt a growing sense of peace about declining the offer and staying where she was. Her decision wasn't easy, but she trusted that God had a greater plan for her. Shortly afterward, an unexpected opportunity arose within her current job—one that allowed her to advance professionally while continuing her ministry work. This confirmation reassured Sarah that seeking God's wisdom had led her to the best choice.

Through this experience, Sarah learned to trust God's timing and guidance. By seeking His wisdom through prayer, Scripture, and godly counsel, she not only found clarity but also deepened her faith. Her decision reminded her that God's wisdom brings peace, even in uncertainty, and equips us to move forward with confidence in His plans.

Small Prayer: Lord, help me to seek Your wisdom in all things. Strengthen my faith and remove any doubts that hinder my trust in You. Amen.

Tuesday: Help My Unbelief

Explanation of Topic: This heartfelt plea reflects the struggle between belief and doubt. It shows that it's okay to ask God for help in overcoming our doubts and growing in faith.

Discussion Question: In what ways does the father's plea in Mark 9:24—"I do believe; help me overcome my unbelief"—resonate with your own experiences of doubt and belief? This heartfelt cry, spoken by a desperate father seeking healing for his son, reveals the tension many of us feel between faith and doubt. It is a raw and honest admission of both trust in God's power and the struggle to fully surrender to it. The father's words remind us that doubt doesn't disqualify us from seeking God's help; instead, it can be a bridge that leads us closer to Him.

Reflect on moments in your life when you've experienced a similar mix of faith and uncertainty. Perhaps you've trusted God's promises but struggled to see how they applied in a challenging situation. Or maybe you believed in His power but found it difficult to trust His timing or methods. The father's plea resonates because it acknowledges that belief and doubt often coexist in the human heart, and it shows that God honors our willingness to bring both to Him.

Consider how this story encourages you to approach God with honesty about your struggles. Have you ever hesitated to pray for fear that your doubts would be seen as a lack of faith? How does Jesus' response to the father—healing his son despite his imperfect faith—reassure you that God meets us where we are, even in our uncertainty?

What practical steps can you take to strengthen your faith in moments of doubt? This might include immersing yourself in Scripture, remembering God's past faithfulness, surrounding yourself with supportive believers, or praying as the father did, asking God to help you believe more fully. How does this story inspire you to trust that God's power is not limited by the strength of your faith but is magnified in your willingness to turn to Him, even when you struggle to fully understand?

Real-World Example: Rachel, a devoted believer, faced a profound crisis of faith after a series of personal hardships. Within the span of a few months, she lost her job, her closest friend moved to another state, and her mother was diagnosed with a serious illness. These events left Rachel feeling abandoned and questioning God's goodness. She still believed in His existence, but she struggled to reconcile her faith with the pain and uncertainty surrounding her. For the first time, she found it difficult to pray or open her Bible, and doubt began to creep into her heart.

One night, overwhelmed by her emotions, Rachel knelt by her bed and prayed, echoing the words of the father in Mark 9:24: "Lord, I do believe; help me overcome my unbelief." It was a raw and honest prayer, admitting both her faith and her struggle. Rachel didn't expect an immediate answer, but she felt a small sense of relief simply by laying her doubts before God.

In the days that followed, Rachel began to seek God intentionally, even in her uncertainty. She committed to reading one Psalm each morning, starting with Psalm 34:18: "The Lord is close to the brokenhearted and saves those who are crushed in spirit." Though she didn't feel an instant change, the verses reminded her that God understood her pain and was near, even when she couldn't sense His presence.

Rachel also reached out to her church community, sharing her struggles with a trusted mentor. Her mentor encouraged her to keep praying, even when it felt difficult, and to look for small signs of God's faithfulness in her daily life. As Rachel followed this advice, she began noticing moments of peace and provision—a friend offering support, an encouraging Scripture verse, and even unexpected financial help during her job search.

Over time, Rachel's faith began to strengthen. Her circumstances didn't change overnight, but her perspective shifted. She learned to trust God in the uncertainty, believing that He was working behind the scenes for her good. This gradual return of peace and trust didn't erase her doubts completely, but it deepened her reliance on God. Rachel's experience taught her that faith isn't the absence of doubt; it's choosing to seek and trust God even in the midst of it.

Small Prayer: Father, I believe; help me overcome my unbelief. Strengthen my faith and guide me through my doubts. Amen.

Wednesday: Jesus' Support

Explanation of Topic: When Peter doubted while walking on water, Jesus immediately helped him. This story illustrates that Jesus is always there to support us, even when we falter in faith

Discussion Question: How does the story of Peter in Matthew 14:31—where Jesus asks, "You of little faith, why did you doubt?"—illustrate Jesus' support during moments of doubt? This story takes place when Peter, full of faith, steps out of the boat to walk on water toward Jesus. At first, Peter does the impossible, walking on the waves with his eyes fixed on Christ. However, when he notices the wind and the waves, fear overtakes him, and he begins to sink. In that moment of doubt, Peter cries out, "Lord, save me!" and Jesus immediately reaches out His hand and catches him.

This story highlights both the reality of human doubt and the steadfastness of Jesus' support. Peter's initial faith demonstrates that trusting Jesus can lead to extraordinary experiences. Yet, his shift in focus—from Jesus to the surrounding storm—shows how easily doubt can creep in when circumstances feel overwhelming. Despite Peter's faltering faith, Jesus doesn't hesitate to rescue him, reinforcing that even in our weakest moments, His grace and presence are constant.

Reflect on how this story resonates with your own life. Have there been times when you stepped out in faith, only to be overcome by fear or doubt when challenges arose? How did those moments affect your relationship with Jesus? Peter's experience reminds us that doubt is not the end of faith; it is an opportunity to reach out to Christ, who is always ready to lift us up.

Consider how keeping your eyes on Jesus—through prayer, Scripture, and worship—can help you remain steadfast, even when life feels turbulent. How does this story encourage you to cry out to Jesus in moments of doubt rather than trying to navigate the storm on your own? Reflect on how Jesus' immediate response to Peter's cry illustrates His willingness to support and strengthen us, reminding us that His power is greater than any storm we face.

Real-World Example: Melissa, a single mother of two, was struggling to balance her responsibilities. Between a demanding job, financial challenges, and caring for her children, she often felt like she was drowning under the weight of it all. Every day brought new stresses—unexpected bills, tight deadlines at work, and the constant pressure to be everything her children needed. Melissa tried to stay strong, but the sleepless nights and endless worries began to take a toll on her emotionally and spiritually. She felt overwhelmed, isolated, and unsure if she could keep going.

One evening, after a particularly exhausting day, Melissa sat alone in her living room, feeling completely defeated. In desperation, she whispered a simple prayer: "Lord, I can't do this on my own. Please help me." It reminded her of Peter's cry in Matthew 14:30: "Lord, save me!" For the first time in weeks, Melissa allowed herself to release her fears and doubts to God, admitting that she needed His support.

In the days that followed, Melissa didn't see an immediate resolution to her problems, but she began to notice subtle changes. A friend unexpectedly offered to help with childcare, easing her workload for a few evenings. Her boss gave her an encouraging compliment, reminding her that her efforts at work were valued. During her morning commute, Melissa started listening to worship music, which brought her a sense of peace and reminded her of God's presence.

As Melissa continued to pray and read Scripture, she felt a gradual shift in her perspective. The challenges in her life didn't disappear, but she no longer felt as though she was facing them alone. She found comfort in verses like Isaiah 41:10: "Do not fear, for I am with you; do not be dismayed, for I am your God." These reminders of God's promises gave her the reassurance she needed to keep moving forward.

Melissa's experience showed her that Jesus doesn't always calm the storm immediately, but He walks with us through it, offering strength and support. Like Peter on the water, Melissa learned that when she kept her focus on Jesus, the overwhelming waves of life became more manageable. Her faith deepened as she realized that even in her weakest moments, Jesus was always there to catch her. This reassurance gave her the courage to face each day with renewed hope and confidence in His presence.

Small Prayer: Jesus, thank You for always being there to catch me when I doubt. Help me to trust in Your support and guidance. Amen.

Thursday: Nature of Faith

Explanation of Topic: Faith involves trust and assurance in things not seen. This verse encourages us to hold onto hope and confidence in God's promises, even amid doubt

Discussion Question: What does Hebrews 11:1—"Now faith is confidence in what we hope for and assurance about what we do not see"—teach us about the nature of faith and its role in addressing doubt?

This verse defines faith as both confidence and assurance, emphasizing trust in God's promises even when they are not immediately visible or tangible. Faith bridges the gap between what we experience in the present and what we believe to be true based on God's Word. It invites us to trust not in what we can see or control but in God's character, sovereignty, and eternal plan.

Reflect on how faith acts as an anchor during times of doubt. Doubt often arises when circumstances feel uncertain or when answers to prayers seem delayed. In these moments, faith provides the assurance that God is working behind the scenes, even when we can't see the outcome. It shifts our focus from our limitations to God's unlimited power and faithfulness, giving us the confidence to persevere.

Faith also reorients our perspective. While doubt can cause us to question God's presence or plan, faith reminds us of His past faithfulness and the hope we have in His promises. Consider how Hebrews 11:1 challenges you to rely on God's track record rather than your immediate circumstances. What specific situations in your life require you to trust in what you cannot see, and how can this definition of faith help you navigate them?

Practical steps to strengthen faith include immersing yourself in Scripture, where God's promises are revealed; engaging in prayer, where you can express your doubts and seek reassurance; and surrounding yourself with a community of believers who can encourage and support you. How might practicing these disciplines help you move from a place of doubt to a deeper, more confident trust in God? Reflect on how living by faith—not by sight—can transform your response to challenges and provide peace in the face of uncertainty.

Real-World Example: Jessica, a devoted believer, had been praying for years for her husband to come to faith in Christ. While she remained committed to her prayers, the lack of visible change in his attitude toward faith often left her feeling discouraged. Her husband, though supportive of her beliefs, showed no interest in attending church or discussing spiritual matters. At times, Jessica wrestled with doubt, wondering if her prayers were making any difference or if God was truly hearing her.

During a Bible study on Hebrews 11:1, Jessica was reminded that faith is not based on immediate results but on confidence in God's promises and assurance in His unseen work. The verse challenged her to trust that God was at work in her husband's life, even if she couldn't see the evidence yet. Jessica began to view her prayers as an act of faith—planting seeds and trusting God for the harvest in His timing.

To strengthen her faith, Jessica immersed herself in Scripture, drawing encouragement from verses like Romans 8:28, which reminds believers that God works all things together for good, and 2 Peter 3:9, which speaks of God's patience in bringing people to repentance. She also sought support from her church community, asking close friends to join her in prayer for her husband. Their encouragement helped her remain hopeful, even on days when doubt crept in.

Jessica also chose to live out her faith with love and grace in her interactions with her husband. She made an effort to reflect Christ's character through her patience, kindness, and unwavering hope. Over time, her husband began to notice the peace and joy that Jessica's faith brought her. Though he didn't immediately embrace her beliefs, his curiosity grew, and he started asking questions about her faith journey.

Years later, Jessica's prayers were answered when her husband decided to attend church with her. He eventually gave his life to Christ, and the moment was a powerful testimony to God's faithfulness. Jessica's unwavering hope and assurance in God's promises, even when no immediate change was visible, not only strengthened her own faith but also played a role in leading her husband to salvation. Her story is a reminder that faith involves trusting in God's unseen work and holding fast to His promises, even when answers seem delayed.

Small Prayer: Lord, give me confidence in what I hope for and assurance in what I do not see. Strengthen my faith and dispel my doubts. Amen.

Friday: Comfort and Reassurance

Explanation of Topic: God's comfort can bring joy even when we are anxious or doubting. Turning to God in times of uncertainty provides peace and reassurance.

Discussion Question: How can Psalm 94:19—"When anxiety was great within me, your consolation brought me joy"—provide comfort and reassurance when you are experiencing spiritual doubt? This verse speaks to God's intimate understanding of our struggles and His ability to bring peace to a restless heart. Doubt often accompanies feelings of anxiety, confusion, or insecurity, especially when we are unsure of God's plans or presence in our lives. However, this Psalm reminds us that in the midst of those feelings, God's consolation—His reassurance, presence, and promises—can bring us joy and restore our confidence in Him.

Reflect on how God's consolation addresses the root of spiritual doubt. When doubt arises, it can feel isolating, as though we are distant from God or forgotten by Him. Yet this verse assures us that God is not only aware of our inner turmoil but actively offers comfort to guide us through it. His Word, His Spirit, and His faithfulness become anchors that steady us when our thoughts are overwhelmed.

Consider how this verse encourages you to turn to God in moments of doubt rather than withdrawing. Have there been times when you felt anxious or uncertain in your faith? What brought you comfort during those seasons? Meditating on Scriptures, worshiping, or recalling God's past faithfulness can help shift your focus from doubt to trust.

Additionally, reflect on the joy mentioned in the verse. This joy isn't rooted in perfect circumstances but in the unchanging nature of God's love and care for us. How might embracing this joy help you move forward with renewed confidence, even when answers to your doubts aren't immediately clear?

Practical steps to find comfort in God's consolation include committing your doubts to prayer, seeking encouragement from mature believers, and spending time reflecting on the promises found in Scripture. How does this verse challenge you to seek God's comfort actively and trust that He is near, offering peace and reassurance even in the midst of uncertainty?

Real-World Example: Rebecca had always considered herself a strong believer, but a series of unexpected events shook her faith. After being laid off from her job, dealing with a health scare, and experiencing a falling-out with a close friend, Rebecca found herself overwhelmed by anxiety. She began questioning God's plans for her life and wondering why her prayers seemed to go unanswered. Her doubts made her feel distant from God, and the weight of uncertainty left her emotionally drained.

One evening, unable to sleep, Rebecca opened her Bible and came across Psalm 94:19: "When anxiety was great within me, your consolation brought me joy." The verse resonated deeply with her, as it acknowledged the reality of her inner turmoil while pointing to God's ability to bring comfort and joy even in the midst of it. Inspired by the verse, Rebecca decided to spend more intentional time with God, bringing her doubts and anxieties to Him in prayer.

Each morning, Rebecca began starting her day with prayer, honestly sharing her fears and uncertainties with God. She also committed to reading a Psalm each day, finding solace in the words of believers who had also struggled with doubt and anxiety yet turned to God for help. As she meditated on Scriptures like Isaiah 41:10—"Do not fear, for I am with you; do not be dismayed, for I am your God"—Rebecca started to feel God's presence more tangibly in her daily life.

Though her circumstances didn't change overnight, Rebecca noticed a gradual shift in her mindset. Her time in prayer and Scripture reading brought a sense of peace that she hadn't felt in months. She began to see small signs of God's faithfulness, such as an encouraging message from a friend, an unexpected job lead, and the strength to handle her health challenges with hope.

Rebecca's anxiety didn't disappear completely, but her trust in God deepened as she leaned on Him daily. The act of bringing her doubts to God not only comforted her but also reminded her that He was in control, working behind the scenes for her good. Through her experience, Rebecca learned that God's presence and promises are powerful sources of reassurance, offering joy and strength even when life feels uncertain.

Small Prayer: Heavenly Father, when anxiety and doubt overwhelm me, bring me Your consolation and joy. Help me to trust in Your peace and comfort. Amen.

End of the Week Closing Prayer for Spiritual Doubt

Heavenly Father,

We humbly come before You, carrying the weight of our doubts and uncertainties. We confess that there are times when our faith feels fragile and our hearts are overwhelmed by questions we cannot answer. Yet, Lord, we know that You are a God of grace and patience, who meets us in our struggles and leads us toward greater understanding and trust.

Strengthen our faith, Lord, and help us to rest in Your wisdom and promises. Teach us to see beyond our circumstances and to trust in Your perfect timing and plan. In our moments of anxiety and doubt, comfort us with Your peace that surpasses all understanding. Remind us that we are never alone and that Your presence surrounds us, even when we cannot see or feel it.

Guide us to a deeper and more resilient faith, one that can withstand life's storms and uncertainties. Help us to grow in confidence, knowing that You are faithful and unchanging. Place supportive and encouraging people in our lives who will walk with us on this journey, offering wisdom, love, and accountability as we seek to grow closer to You.

Fill our hearts with the assurance of Your presence, Lord, and the joy of knowing that You are always with us. Thank You for Your endless patience, Your unfailing love, and Your desire to draw us closer to You, even when we falter.

In Jesus' name, we pray. Amen

Week 13: Spiritual Distress

Introduction

Spiritual distress can occur when someone struggles to find meaning, peace, strength, connection, or comfort in life. This condition can manifest through feelings of anger, depression, anxiety, hopelessness, difficulty sleeping, and a sense of abandonment by God. The Bible offers comfort, guidance, and hope for those experiencing spiritual distress, helping them to reconnect with God and find solace in His promises.

Definition

Spiritual Distress: A condition characterized by an inability to find meaning, peace, strength, connection, or comfort in life, often accompanied by feelings of anger, depression, anxiety, hopelessness, difficulty sleeping, and a sense of abandonment by God.

Key Scriptures

Psalm 34:17-18 (NIV)-"The righteous cry out, and the Lord hears them; he delivers them from all their troubles. The Lord is close to the brokenhearted and saves those who are crushed in spirit."

Philippians 4:6-7 (NIV)-"Do not be anxious about anything, but in every situation, by prayer and petition, with thanksgiving, present your requests to God. And the peace of God, which transcends all understanding, will guard your hearts and your minds in Christ Jesus."

Isaiah 41:10 (NIV)-"So do not fear, for I am with you; do not be dismayed, for I am your God. I will strengthen you and help you; I will uphold you with my righteous right hand."

Matthew 11:28-30 (NIV)-"Come to me, all you who are weary and burdened, and I will give you rest. Take my yoke upon you and learn from me, for I am gentle and humble in heart, and you will find rest for your souls. For my yoke is easy and my burden is light."

Psalm 23:1-4 (NIV)-"The Lord is my shepherd, I lack nothing. He makes me lie down in green pastures, he leads me beside quiet waters, he refreshes my soul. He guides me along the right paths for his name's sake. Even though I walk through the darkest valley, I will fear no evil, for you are with me; your rod and your staff, they comfort me."

Monday: God is Close to the Brokenhearted

Explanation of Topic: God hears the cries of the distressed and promises to be near to the brokenhearted. This verse reassures us that God is present and attentive to our suffering.

Discussion Question: How does knowing that God is close to the brokenhearted, as expressed in Psalm 34:18—"The Lord is close to the brokenhearted and saves those who are crushed in spirit"—bring comfort during times of spiritual distress? This verse reminds us of God's intimate presence in our moments of deepest pain and struggle. It assures us that when we feel broken, overwhelmed, or spiritually lost, God doesn't distance Himself from us. Instead, He draws near, offering His comfort, love, and salvation.

Spiritual distress often comes with feelings of isolation, as though no one truly understands the depth of our pain. This verse counters those feelings by affirming that God not only understands but is actively present with us in our suffering. His closeness provides a source of strength and hope, reminding us that we are not abandoned, even when life feels unbearable.

Consider how this truth changes the way you view difficult times. Have you ever felt brokenhearted or crushed in spirit? How did the awareness of God's presence—or the lack of it—impact your ability to endure and heal? Reflect on how His closeness can provide reassurance, even when your circumstances remain challenging.

This verse also speaks to God's power to save and restore. He doesn't just stand beside us in our distress; He actively works to bring healing and renewal. Think about how trusting in God's nearness can help you take steps toward recovery, whether through prayer, leaning on His promises, or seeking support from a faith community.

How might embracing this truth deepen your relationship with God? Reflect on how His closeness during spiritual distress can strengthen your faith and encourage you to trust Him more fully. How can this verse inspire you to seek Him in your brokenness, knowing that His love is unwavering and His power to heal is limitless?

Real-World Example: Maria had always relied on her faith to guide her through life's challenges, but when she unexpectedly lost her mother, the grief was overwhelming. The pain of the loss left her feeling crushed in spirit, and she found it difficult to pray or find comfort in the usual ways. Her days felt heavy and unending, and her nights were filled with tears and questions. She wondered why God had allowed her mother to be taken so soon and felt as though her faith was being tested like never before.

One evening, while sitting alone with her Bible, Maria came across Psalm 34:18: "The Lord is close to the brokenhearted and saves those who are crushed in spirit." The words seemed to leap off the page, resonating deeply with her. For the first time since her mother's passing, Maria allowed herself to sit in God's presence without needing to find answers. She realized that God wasn't asking her to "fix" her grief but was offering to walk with her through it.

Encouraged by this promise, Maria began to talk to God openly about her pain. She started journaling her prayers, pouring out her sorrow and doubts, and asking for His comfort and strength. Though the pain didn't disappear, she began to sense a quiet assurance that she wasn't alone. Small moments of solace appeared—an encouraging word from a friend, a song at church that reminded her of God's love, and memories of her mother that brought both tears and gratitude.

Maria also reached out to her church's grief support group, where she found others who had experienced similar losses. Sharing her story and hearing theirs helped her feel less isolated. She discovered that God's presence often came through the kindness and empathy of those around her. Slowly, her heart began to heal, and she found moments of peace amidst her grief.

Through this journey, Maria learned that God's closeness doesn't always erase the pain but provides strength to endure it. Knowing that He was present in her darkest moments gave her hope and reassurance, reminding her that His love was constant, even in loss. This understanding deepened Maria's faith, helping her trust that God was with her not only in her joy but also in her brokenness.

Explanation of Topic: God hears the cries of the distressed and promises to be near to the brokenhearted. This verse reassures us that God is present and attentive to our suffering.

Small Prayer: Lord, I am hurting and brokenhearted. Please be close to me, comfort me, and deliver me from my troubles. Amen.

Tuesday: Handling Anxiety with God's Peace

Explanation of Topic: Through prayer and thanksgiving, we can present our anxieties to God and receive His peace. This passage encourages us to trust in God's provision and find peace in His presence.

Discussion Question: In what ways does Philippians 4:6-7—"Do not be anxious about anything, but in every situation, by prayer and petition, with thanksgiving, present your requests to God. And the peace of God, which transcends all understanding, will guard your hearts and your minds in Christ Jesus"—encourage you to handle anxiety and seek God's peace?

This passage provides a clear blueprint for addressing anxiety, reminding us that we don't need to face our worries alone. Instead of letting anxiety overwhelm us, Paul encourages us to turn every situation over to God through prayer and petition. By presenting our concerns to Him, we acknowledge our dependence on His power and wisdom, trusting that He cares for us and is in control.

The verse also emphasizes the importance of gratitude in the midst of prayer. When we approach God with thanksgiving, we shift our focus from what is lacking or uncertain to what He has already provided. This practice helps to combat anxiety by reminding us of His past faithfulness and the blessings in our lives, reinforcing our confidence in His ability to handle whatever we are facing.

The promise in this passage is profound: when we bring our anxieties to God, His peace, which surpasses human understanding, will guard our hearts and minds. This peace is not dependent on the resolution of our circumstances but flows from knowing that God is with us and that He is greater than our worries. It provides a sense of calm and security that transcends logic or explanation, allowing us to rest in His presence even when life feels uncertain.

Reflect on how you can apply these principles in your own life. Are there specific anxieties you have been holding onto instead of surrendering to God in prayer? How might incorporating gratitude into your prayers change your perspective and help you find peace? Consider how this passage challenges you to trust God's promise to guard your heart and mind, allowing His peace to replace your anxiety.

Finally, think about how experiencing God's peace can impact not only your own well-being but also your relationships with others. How might modeling a calm and trusting spirit encourage those around you to seek God's peace in their own lives? This verse invites you to experience the transformative power of prayer and gratitude, leading to a deeper connection with God and His perfect peace.

Real-World Example: Jacob was a young professional navigating a stressful season in his life. He was juggling long hours at work, mounting financial responsibilities, and concerns about his aging parents' health. Each day felt like a relentless wave of pressure, leaving him overwhelmed and unable to focus. Jacob's anxiety began to affect his sleep, his relationships, and even his ability to enjoy activities he once loved. He felt like he was spiraling, unsure how to regain control of his thoughts and emotions.

One evening, Jacob confided in a trusted friend from his church. His friend shared Philippians 4:6-7 with him, encouraging Jacob to bring all of his worries to God in prayer. Although skeptical about whether prayer could ease his burdens, Jacob decided to give it a try. That night, he sat in his living room, took a deep breath, and began to talk to God. He poured out every concern—his fears about work, his financial struggles, and his worry for his parents' well-being. As he prayed, he also made an effort to express gratitude for the blessings in his life: a supportive family, a roof over his head, and the strength to get through each day.

As Jacob continued this practice each evening, something unexpected happened. While his external circumstances hadn't changed, he began to feel a sense of calm during and after his prayer times. It was as if a weight had been lifted off his shoulders. He realized that by surrendering his anxieties to God, he was acknowledging that he didn't have to face his challenges alone. He found comfort in the promise that God was in control, even when life felt chaotic.

In addition to prayer, Jacob started meditating on Scriptures that reinforced God's faithfulness, such as Isaiah 26:3: "You will keep in perfect peace those whose minds are steadfast, because they trust in you." These verses became an anchor for him, reminding him to refocus on God rather than his worries. Over time, Jacob's ability to cope with stress improved. He began sleeping better, his relationships felt more balanced, and he approached his responsibilities with a renewed sense of energy and trust.

Jacob's experience taught him that God's peace, as described in Philippians 4:7, truly transcends understanding. While his challenges didn't disappear, his reliance on prayer and God's promises transformed how he navigated them. This peace became a testimony to those around him, inspiring his friends and family to seek God in their own moments of anxiety and uncertainty.

Small Prayer: Heavenly Father, I bring my anxieties to You. Fill me with Your peace that transcends all understanding and guard my heart and mind. Amen.

Wednesday: Strength and Reassurance in God

Explanation of Topic: God promises His presence, strength, and help. This verse offers assurance that we are not alone in our distress and that God is our support

Discussion Question: How can Isaiah 41:10—"So do not fear, for I am with you; do not be dismayed, for I am your God. I will strengthen you and help you; I will uphold you with my righteous right hand"—strengthen your faith and provide reassurance when you feel overwhelmed?

This powerful verse serves as a direct reminder of God's presence, strength, and commitment to His people during times of fear and uncertainty. It begins with a clear command: "Do not fear." While fear and overwhelm are natural responses to life's challenges, God reassures us that we are not alone. His presence is constant, and His sovereignty is greater than any obstacle we face. This knowledge encourages us to replace fear with trust in His unchanging character.

The phrase "Do not be dismayed, for I am your God" highlights God's personal relationship with us. It is not a distant or impersonal assurance, but one rooted in the reality that He is our loving and faithful God. This relationship is the foundation for trusting Him to provide strength and guidance when we feel weak and uncertain.

God's promise to "strengthen you and help you" reinforces that He doesn't just watch from afar but actively participates in our struggles. His strength is made available to us in moments of overwhelm, giving us the ability to endure and move forward. The imagery of being upheld by His "righteous right hand" is especially powerful—it conveys a sense of protection, stability, and unwavering support. Even when we feel like we are sinking under the weight of our circumstances, God promises to sustain us and hold us steady.

Reflect on how this verse applies to your own life. Have there been times when you felt overwhelmed, either by external challenges or internal fears? How did remembering God's presence and promises help you navigate those moments? Consider how this verse invites you to shift your focus from the size of your problem to the greatness of your God.

Practical steps to internalize this reassurance might include memorizing this verse and meditating on it during stressful times, praying it back to God when you feel overwhelmed, or journaling about specific ways you've seen Him strengthen and uphold you in the past. How does embracing the truths of Isaiah 41:10 help you build resilience and confidence, knowing that God's power and presence are always with you? Reflect on how this assurance can transform fear into faith and discouragement into hope.

Real-World Example: David, a devoted husband and father, was blindsided when his employer announced massive layoffs at the company where he had worked for over a decade. The loss of his job left him reeling with a mix of fear, uncertainty, and self-doubt. As the primary breadwinner for his family, David felt the weight of responsibility pressing down on him. He questioned how he would provide for his family and whether he would find another position in such an unstable job market.

In the midst of his anxiety, David turned to his Bible for reassurance and came across Isaiah 41:10: "So do not fear, for I am with you; do not be dismayed, for I am your God. I will strengthen you and help you; I will uphold you with my righteous right hand." The verse struck a chord with him, offering a glimmer of hope in his darkest moment. David decided to hold onto this promise, trusting that God's strength and support would sustain him as he faced this uncertain chapter in his life.

Each morning, David began his day with prayer, asking God for guidance, strength, and peace. He also shared his struggles with his small group at church, where he received encouragement and practical advice from others who had faced similar challenges. As he applied for jobs and prepared for interviews, David meditated on Isaiah 41:10, reminding himself that he was not alone and that God was actively working in his situation.

Though the job search was not without its setbacks, David noticed that his outlook began to shift. Instead of succumbing to fear and discouragement, he felt a growing sense of peace and determination. God's promises gave him the courage to persevere, even when the process felt slow and uncertain. He also found opportunities to grow spiritually, using the extra time to deepen his prayer life and reflect on how God had been faithful in the past.

Several weeks later, David received a job offer that was better than he had hoped for—one that provided financial stability and allowed him to spend more time with his family. Reflecting on his journey, David realized that the experience, though difficult, had strengthened his faith and deepened his dependence on God. Isaiah 41:10 had become a source of comfort and reassurance, reminding him that God's strength and support were constant, even in the face of life's most overwhelming challenges.

David's story serves as a testament to the power of trusting in God's promises. By leaning on His Word, seeking support from his faith community, and relying on prayer, David was able to face an uncertain future with hope and confidence, knowing that God was upholding him every step of the way.

Small Prayer: God, I feel overwhelmed and fearful. Strengthen me, help me, and uphold me with Your righteous right hand. Amen.

Thursday: Rest for the Weary

Explanation of Topic: Jesus invites those who are weary to come to Him for rest. His gentleness and humility provide comfort and relief from our burdens

Discussion Question: How does Matthew 11:28-30—"Come to me, all you who are weary and burdened, and I will give you rest. Take my yoke upon you and learn from me, for I am gentle and humble in heart, and you will find rest for your souls. For my yoke is easy and my burden is light"—offer relief and rest from the burdens of life? How can you practically come to Jesus with your weariness?

This passage reveals the heart of Jesus as a compassionate and approachable Savior who invites us to bring our struggles, weariness, and burdens to Him. Life often overwhelms us with responsibilities, uncertainties, and challenges that drain our energy and spirit. Jesus acknowledges this reality and offers a solution: to come to Him and exchange our heavy burdens for His light yoke.

The imagery of the yoke is significant. A yoke, traditionally used to pair oxen together, symbolizes work and guidance. By taking on Jesus' yoke, we are invited to walk alongside Him, allowing Him to guide and share the weight of our burdens. His yoke is "easy" not because life becomes free of challenges but because His presence and strength enable us to endure with peace and hope. Jesus' humility and gentleness assure us that He will meet us with understanding and love, not judgment or condemnation, regardless of our struggles.

Reflect on how this invitation applies to your life. What are the specific burdens or sources of weariness that you are carrying? How might releasing those burdens to Jesus provide relief and rest for your soul? Consider the ways in which trying to carry these burdens alone has affected your emotional, physical, or spiritual well-being.

Practically coming to Jesus involves intentional steps of surrender and trust. This might include setting aside time each day to pray and honestly share your concerns with Him, meditating on Scriptures that remind you of His faithfulness, or finding community within the church to support and pray with you. It also means choosing to trust His timing and plan, even when the path ahead feels unclear.

How can adopting Jesus' yoke reshape your perspective on life's challenges? Reflect on how His strength, guidance, and peace can replace feelings of exhaustion and hopelessness with renewed energy and purpose. Discuss how this passage invites you to not only rest in His presence but also learn from Him, growing in faith and reliance on His unchanging character.

Real-World Example: Lisa, a working mother of three, often felt overwhelmed by the endless demands of her life. Between managing her full-time job, supporting her children's school activities, and caring for her aging parents, Lisa was stretched thin. Each day felt like a race against the clock, leaving her physically exhausted and emotionally drained. Despite her best efforts to stay positive, she often found herself on the verge of tears, wondering how long she could keep going at this pace.

One Sunday, during a church service, the pastor preached on Matthew 11:28-30: "Come to me, all you who are weary and burdened, and I will give you rest." As Lisa listened, she realized that she had been trying to carry all her burdens on her own without turning to Jesus for help. The verse's promise of rest and renewal resonated deeply with her, and she felt an invitation to let go of her self-reliance and seek God's strength.

That evening, Lisa sat down in her living room after the kids were asleep, opened her Bible, and began to pray. She poured out her heart to Jesus, listing each burden she was carrying—her worries about work, her guilt over not spending enough time with her children, and her fears about her parents' health. For the first time in weeks, she allowed herself to cry, releasing the pent-up frustration and exhaustion. She asked Jesus to guide her, to lighten her load, and to give her the rest her soul desperately needed.

In the days that followed, Lisa made small but intentional changes to invite Jesus into her daily life. She started her mornings with a short prayer, asking for wisdom and strength for the day ahead. During her commute, she listened to worship music, which helped her focus on God's presence instead of her to-do list. She also began meditating on Scriptures like Philippians 4:13: "I can do all this through him who gives me strength."

Gradually, Lisa noticed a change. While her responsibilities remained the same, her perspective shifted. She no longer felt as though she had to bear every burden alone. Jesus' promise of rest gave her permission to pause, breathe, and trust that He was walking beside her. Small moments of peace—like a kind word from a coworker, a hug from her children, or an answered prayer for her parents—reminded her of God's faithfulness.

Lisa's experience taught her that Jesus' rest wasn't just about physical relief but a deeper sense of renewal in her spirit. By surrendering her burdens to Him, she found strength she didn't know she had and a renewed sense of purpose. Lisa's journey became a testimony to those around her, showing that even in the busiest seasons of life, turning to Jesus can bring the peace and rest that our souls long for.

Small Prayer: Jesus, I am weary and burdened. I come to You for rest. Teach me to trust in Your gentleness and find rest for my soul. Amen.

Friday: God's Provision and Comfort

Explanation of Topic: God, as our shepherd, provides for our needs, refreshes our soul, and comforts us in dark times. This psalm reminds us of God's constant care and guidance.

Discussion Question: How does Psalm 23:1-4—"The Lord is my shepherd, I lack nothing. He makes me lie down in green pastures, he leads me beside quiet waters, he refreshes my soul. He guides me along the right paths for his name's sake. Even though I walk through the darkest valley, I will fear no evil, for you are with me; your rod and your staff, they comfort me"—illustrate God's provision, guidance, and comfort in times of distress?

This beloved passage paints a vivid picture of God's care, depicting Him as a shepherd who tends to every need of His flock. It highlights three key aspects of His character that provide reassurance in moments of distress: His provision, guidance, and comfort.

Provision: The psalm begins with the assurance that with the Lord as our shepherd, we lack nothing. This doesn't mean that we will always have everything we want, but rather that God provides everything we need to thrive spiritually, emotionally, and physically. The imagery of green pastures and quiet waters symbolizes rest, nourishment, and peace. Even in the midst of chaos, God offers a place of renewal and refreshment for our weary souls.

Guidance: As a shepherd, God leads us along the right paths. His guidance isn't arbitrary but is grounded in His perfect knowledge and character. Even when the path ahead seems uncertain or difficult, we can trust that He is directing our steps for His glory and our good. This verse challenges us to rely on His wisdom rather than our own understanding, recognizing that His ways lead to life and peace.

Comfort: The promise of God's presence in the darkest valleys is one of the most profound aspects of this psalm. Valleys symbolize times of fear, danger, or uncertainty, yet the psalmist declares, "I will fear no evil, for you are with me." God's presence provides courage and reassurance, reminding us that we are never alone. The rod and staff, tools of the shepherd, symbolize protection and guidance, assuring us that God is both defending us from harm and keeping us on the right path.

Reflect on how these truths apply to your own life. Have there been times when you experienced God's provision during a season of need? How has His guidance brought clarity to a situation that felt uncertain? How does His presence comfort you in moments of fear or distress?

Practically, embracing the truths of Psalm 23:1-4 might involve meditating on its promises during challenging times, praying for God's guidance and provision, or recalling specific instances when He has been faithful in the past. How does understanding God as your shepherd encourage you to trust Him more fully, even in the valleys of life? Reflect on how His provision, guidance, and comfort can transform distress into peace and assurance.

Real-World Example: Emily had always leaned on her faith, but when she entered one of the most challenging seasons of her life, she felt lost and unsure of how to move forward. Within a span of months, she lost her job, faced a serious health diagnosis, and had to care for her aging father, whose condition was deteriorating rapidly. Overwhelmed by the weight of her responsibilities and the uncertainty of the future, Emily often cried out to God, asking why everything was happening at once. She felt like she was walking through a dark valley with no end in sight.

One evening, during a particularly difficult day, Emily opened her Bible to Psalm 23. As she read the familiar words, they took on a new depth of meaning: "The Lord is my shepherd, I lack nothing." She realized that even though her circumstances felt overwhelming, God was still present, providing for her in ways she hadn't noticed. Reflecting on the past few months, Emily saw how her friends had supported her with meals, prayers, and encouragement. She also remembered how her medical team had been attentive and compassionate throughout her health journey.

These moments of provision reminded her that God was caring for her, even in the valley.

The phrase "He makes me lie down in green pastures" resonated deeply with Emily. She realized that she hadn't allowed herself to rest, feeling as though she had to keep pushing forward on her own strength. Inspired by the psalm, she started setting aside time each day to pray, meditate on Scripture, and rest in God's presence. This practice brought her moments of peace and refreshed her spirit, helping her face each day with renewed strength.

The promise of God's guidance—"He guides me along the right paths for his name's sake"—gave Emily hope that she wasn't navigating this season alone. She prayed for wisdom in making decisions about her father's care and her next steps after losing her job. Over time, she began to see how God was gently leading her, opening doors for a part-time remote job that allowed her to balance work and caregiving.

Finally, the words "Even though I walk through the darkest valley, I will fear no evil, for you are with me" reminded Emily that God's presence was constant, even in her deepest struggles. When fear and anxiety crept in, she would repeat this verse, visualizing God walking beside her, protecting and guiding her with His rod and staff. This assurance gave her courage to keep going, even when the path ahead seemed uncertain.

Emily's journey through her dark valley wasn't easy, but Psalm 23 became a lifeline that helped her rediscover God's care and guidance. She found comfort in His provision, strength in His presence, and hope in His promises. Her experience reminded her that no matter how difficult the season, God, as her shepherd, was always there to lead her to green pastures, quiet waters, and ultimately, restoration.

Small Prayer: Lord, You are my shepherd. Thank You for providing for my needs, guiding me, and comforting me in dark times. Amen.

End of the Week Closing Prayer for Spiritual Distress

Heavenly Father,

We come before You with humble hearts, bringing the weight of our spiritual distress and burdens to Your feet. In our moments of brokenness, we seek Your comfort and peace, knowing that You are near to the brokenhearted and attentive to the cries of Your children. Thank You for being a God who does not abandon us in our struggles but instead walks with us through the valleys, offering Your unwavering presence and love.

Strengthen us, Lord, when we feel weak and overwhelmed. Remind us that You are our Shepherd, guiding us along the right paths and providing for all our needs. Help us to trust in Your care, even when the way forward is unclear. Let the promises of Your Word be our anchor, assuring us that You will never leave nor forsake us and that Your plans for us are filled with hope and purpose.

As we face the challenges of life, teach us to rest in Jesus, who invites us to cast our burdens on Him and promises to give rest to our weary souls. Refresh us daily with Your Spirit, filling us with the peace that surpasses all understanding. Let us find joy in Your presence, even amid trials, and may Your comfort renew our strength to face each day.

Lord, we ask for Your guidance as we navigate difficult seasons. Uphold us with Your righteous right hand and lead us to a deeper faith and trust in You. Let our lives reflect Your grace and mercy so that others may see Your light shining through us.

We thank You for Your faithfulness, Your love, and Your never-ending care. In the name of Jesus, who carries our burdens and grants us peace, we pray. Amen.

Week 14: Spiritual Depression

Introduction

Spiritual depression is a condition where individuals feel disconnected or cut off from God. This experience can lead to confusion, frustration, and a sense of being unable to communicate with God, often accompanied by the belief that God no longer hears their prayers. The Bible provides guidance, comfort, and hope for those struggling with spiritual depression, helping them to restore their connection with God and find peace.

Definition

Spiritual Depression: A condition characterized by feelings of disconnection or being cut off from God, often accompanied by confusion, frustration, and a belief that God no longer hears one's prayers.

Key Scriptures

Psalm 42:1-3 (NIV)-"As the deer pants for streams of water, so my soul pants for you, my God. My soul thirsts for God, for the living God. When can I go and meet with God? My tears have been my food day and night, while people say to me all day long, 'Where is your God?'"

Psalm 77:1-3 (NIV)-"I cried out to God for help; I cried out to God to hear me. When I was in distress, I sought the Lord; at night I stretched out untiring hands, and I would not be comforted. I remembered you, God, and I groaned; I meditated, and my spirit grew faint."

Lamentations 3:22-24 (NIV)-"Because of the Lord's great love we are not consumed, for his compassions never fail. They are new every morning; great is your faithfulness. I say to myself, 'The Lord is my portion; therefore, I will wait for him.'"

Matthew 11:28-30 (NIV)-"Come to me, all you who are weary and burdened, and I will give you rest. Take my yoke upon you and learn from me, for I am gentle and humble in heart, and you will find rest for your souls. For my yoke is easy and my burden is light."

Romans 8:38-39 (NIV)-"For I am convinced that neither death nor life, neither angels nor demons, neither the present nor the future, nor any powers, neither height nor depth, nor anything else in all creation, will be able to separate us from the love of God that is in Christ Jesus our Lord."

Monday: Longing for God

Explanation of Topic: The psalmist's deep thirst for God and lament over feeling distant from Him resonates with those experiencing spiritual depression. It reminds us that expressing our longing and pain to God is a step toward healing.

Discussion Question: How does the psalmist's deep longing for God, as expressed in Psalm 42:1-3—"As the deer pants for streams of water, so my soul pants for you, my God. My soul thirsts for God, for the living God. When can I go and meet with God? My tears have been my food day and night, while people say to me all day long, 'Where is your God?'"—resonate with your experience of spiritual depression?

This psalm vividly portrays the anguish of spiritual depression—a state where God's presence feels distant and life feels heavy with sorrow. The psalmist's longing for God is compared to a parched deer desperately seeking water, symbolizing an intense need for spiritual renewal and connection. This deep thirst for God resonates with those who feel disconnected from Him, where prayer feels empty, worship seems hollow, and the joy of faith feels out of reach.

Reflect on moments in your life when you've felt a similar longing. Have there been times when you've experienced a dryness in your spiritual life, where God's presence felt distant despite your desire to draw near? How did that sense of distance affect your emotions, actions, and faith journey? The psalmist's words remind us that it's normal to experience seasons of spiritual drought and that even in our most painful moments, our longing for God reflects the authenticity of our faith.

The psalm also acknowledges the external pressures that compound spiritual depression, such as the doubts or criticisms of others—"Where is your God?" These voices can deepen feelings of isolation and despair, making it harder to cling to God's promises. How do you respond to such challenges, and how can remembering God's faithfulness in the past help you counter these doubts?

Practical steps to address spiritual depression might include honest prayer, as the psalmist models, expressing your struggles directly to God without fear of judgment. Meditating on Scriptures that emphasize God's closeness, such as Psalm 34:18—"The Lord is close to the brokenhearted"—can also bring comfort. Additionally, seeking encouragement from a supportive faith community or trusted mentor can help reignite hope and remind you that you're not alone in your journey.

How does the psalmist's longing for God inspire you to keep seeking Him, even when He feels distant? Reflect on how this passage encourages you to trust that your spiritual thirst will ultimately be quenched by God's presence and that even in your deepest struggles, He is drawing you closer to Him.

Real-World Example: James had been a faithful churchgoer for years. He attended services every Sunday, participated in Bible studies, and even served on the worship team. Outwardly, everything seemed fine, but inside, James felt spiritually dry and distant from God. Despite his involvement in church activities, his prayers felt hollow, and his Bible reading had become more of a routine than a source of inspiration. He began to question whether God was really present in his life and wondered why he felt so disconnected despite doing everything "right."

The turning point came one evening after a particularly busy day. Exhausted and discouraged, James stumbled upon Psalm 42:1-3: "As the deer pants for streams of water, so my soul pants for you, my God." The words struck a chord, perfectly capturing the emptiness he felt. For the first time in months, James acknowledged to himself—and to God—that he was struggling spiritually. He prayed honestly, admitting his feelings of dryness and asking for help to reconnect with God.

Determined to address his spiritual state, James made changes to his routine. Instead of simply reading the Bible to check it off his to-do list, he began meditating on small passages, asking God to speak to him through His Word. He also set aside dedicated time for silent prayer and reflection, allowing himself to sit quietly in God's presence without an agenda. These moments, though challenging at first, helped James reconnect with the simplicity and intimacy of his relationship with God.

James also sought support from his small group, sharing his struggles openly for the first time. To his surprise, several others in the group admitted they had experienced similar seasons of spiritual dryness. Their honesty and encouragement reminded James that he wasn't alone in his journey. They prayed for him, shared their own strategies for reigniting their faith, and invited him to join a retreat focused on spiritual renewal.

Gradually, James began to feel his spiritual thirst being quenched. He found joy in prayer again and started noticing God's presence in his daily life—in the beauty of creation, in the words of a worship song, and in the small acts of kindness from those around him. Though the dryness didn't disappear overnight, James discovered that his longing for God had drawn him closer to Him. The season of spiritual distance became a time of growth, teaching him that faith isn't just about outward practices but about continually seeking a deeper connection with God.

James's story reminds us that spiritual dryness doesn't mean God is absent. Sometimes, it's an invitation to slow down, refocus, and rediscover the richness of His presence. Through honesty, intentional practices, and the support of community, James found renewal and a deeper understanding of God's faithfulness.

Small Prayer: Lord, I feel distant and disconnected from You. Please draw near to me and fill my heart with Your presence. Amen.

Tuesday: Persisting in Seeking God

Explanation of Topic: This passage highlights the psalmist's distress and persistent seeking of God despite feeling unheard. It reflects the struggle and determination to connect with God during times of spiritual depression.

Discussion Question: How does Psalm 77:1-3—"I cried out to God for help; I cried out to God to hear me. When I was in distress, I sought the Lord; at night I stretched out untiring hands, and I would not be comforted. I remembered you, God, and I groaned; I meditated, and my spirit grew faint"—encourage you to persist in seeking God despite feeling unheard?

These verses vividly capture the psalmist's experience of crying out to God in a season of distress and feeling as though there is no response. It reflects the raw emotions that many believers experience during times of spiritual struggle—moments of desperation, frustration, and even exhaustion in prayer. Yet, despite these feelings, the psalmist continues to seek God, demonstrating a steadfast faith that refuses to give up, even when comfort seems far away.

This passage encourages us to be honest with God about our struggles. The psalmist doesn't hide his pain or pretend to have everything together; instead, he openly expresses his distress. This teaches us that bringing our unfiltered emotions to God is an act of faith in itself, showing that we trust Him enough to share our deepest pain. How does this example challenge you to persist in prayer, even when it feels difficult or unproductive?

The psalmist's persistence is also evident in his actions: stretching out untiring hands, meditating, and remembering God. These practices reflect a determination to remain connected to God, even when His presence feels distant. Consider how incorporating similar practices— such as consistent prayer, meditating on Scripture, or reflecting on God's past faithfulness—can help you stay grounded in your faith during times of spiritual silence.

Reflect on how God's timing and ways often differ from our expectations. Have there been times in your life when you felt unheard in prayer, only to later realize that God was working behind the scenes? How does this passage encourage you to trust that God is still listening and caring for you, even when you can't immediately see the results?

Finally, think about how persistence in seeking God transforms not only your circumstances but also your character. What steps can you take to remain faithful in your pursuit of Him, and how might this deepen your relationship with Him over time? Psalm 77:1-3 reminds us that persistence in seeking God, even amid silence, is a powerful expression of trust and a pathway to eventual renewal and comfort.

Real-World Example:

Maria had always been a passionate believer, deeply involved in her church and personal prayer life. But over time, she began to feel spiritually dry.

Her once-vibrant faith seemed distant, and she struggled to sense God's presence. Maria continued to pray daily, but her words felt hollow, and her Bible reading seemed like an empty routine. She questioned whether God was truly listening and wondered if her faith had become stagnant.

Despite her feelings of distance, Maria clung to the promise that God never abandons His children. She drew strength from Psalm 77:1-3, which echoed her own experience: "I cried out to God for help; I cried out to God to hear me. When I was in distress, I sought the Lord." This passage encouraged her to persist in seeking God, even when her prayers seemed unanswered.

Each morning, Maria began her day by crying out to God in honesty, expressing her frustration and longing for renewal. She started journaling her prayers, documenting her feelings, and reminding herself of the times God had been faithful in her past. On particularly challenging days, she would revisit these entries, finding hope in how God had previously worked in her life.

Maria also sought support from her small group, sharing her struggle with spiritual dryness. Her vulnerability inspired others in the group to share their own similar experiences. Together, they prayed for one another and exchanged practical ideas for rekindling their faith, such as trying new ways to engage with Scripture or spending time in nature to connect with God's creation.

Maria also committed to incorporating worship music into her daily routine. Listening to songs that focused on God's character and promises helped her refocus her heart on His goodness, even when she couldn't feel it. Over time, this practice began to soften her heart, allowing her to experience small moments of connection with God.

Though the season of spiritual dryness didn't resolve immediately, Maria noticed subtle changes. She began to feel a renewed sense of peace during her prayer times and found herself genuinely moved by Scriptures that once felt routine. God's presence became more tangible as she persisted in seeking Him, teaching her that faith isn't dependent on feelings but on trust in His unchanging character.

Maria's journey reminded her that spiritual dryness is often a refining process, drawing believers closer to God as they learn to rely on Him fully. Her persistence in prayer and commitment to seeking God helped her emerge from this season with a deeper, more resilient faith. Her story became an encouragement to others, showing that God is always present, even in the silence, and that He honors those who seek Him with all their hearts.

Small Prayer: Heavenly Father, even when I feel unheard, help me to continue seeking You. Strengthen my spirit and let me find solace in Your presence. Amen.

Wednesday: Hope and Reassurance in God's Faithfulness

Explanation of Topic: Despite the feelings of despair, this scripture reminds us of God's unfailing love and faithfulness. It encourages hope and trust in God's compassionate nature.

Discussion Question: How does Lamentations 3:22-24—"Because of the Lord's great love we are not consumed, for his compassions never fail. They are new every morning; great is your faithfulness. I say to myself, 'The Lord is my portion; therefore I will wait for him.'"—offer hope and reassurance during times of despair?

This passage, written during one of the darkest periods in Israel's history, reflects a profound hope rooted in the unchanging character of God. Despite the author's grief and the overwhelming circumstances surrounding him, these verses affirm that God's love, mercy, and faithfulness remain constant. They provide a powerful reminder that despair doesn't have the final word—God's compassion and presence do.

The phrase "Because of the Lord's great love we are not consumed" reassures us that no matter how overwhelming our struggles may feel, God's love sustains us. This love is not fleeting or conditional but enduring and steadfast. Reflect on moments in your own life when you felt like you couldn't go on, yet somehow found the strength to keep moving forward. How does knowing that God's love is your foundation give you the resilience to face despair?

The promise that God's compassions "never fail" and are "new every morning" reminds us that each day is an opportunity for renewal. Even when yesterday was filled with sorrow or failure, God's mercy meets us afresh each morning. How might adopting this perspective help you approach each day with renewed hope, even in difficult seasons?

The declaration "The Lord is my portion" speaks to a deep trust in God as the ultimate source of satisfaction and provision. In times of despair, when it's tempting to seek comfort in temporary solutions, this verse challenges us to rely fully on God. How can you make Him your portion—your source of hope and strength—amid life's hardships?

Finally, the commitment to "wait for him" emphasizes patience and trust in God's timing. In despair, waiting can feel unbearable, but this passage assures us that God's faithfulness is worth the wait. Reflect on how trusting in God's timing, rather than seeking immediate answers, can provide peace and reassurance.

Lamentations 3:22-24 invites us to shift our focus from our circumstances to the unwavering character of God. How does embracing His great love, unfailing compassion, and daily renewal transform your perspective during times of despair? What steps can you take to remind yourself of these truths and anchor your hope in His faithfulness?

Real World Example: Someone finding hope in God's faithfulness and compassion during a difficult personal crisis.

Small Prayer: Lord, remind me of Your great love and compassion. Help me to trust in Your faithfulness and find hope in Your promises. Amen.

Thursday: Rest for the Weary

Explanation of Topic: Jesus invites those who are weary and burdened to find rest in Him. This passage offers comfort and reassurance that Jesus understands our struggles and provides rest for our souls.

Discussion Question: How does Matthew 11:28-30—"Come to me, all you who are weary and burdened, and I will give you rest. Take my yoke upon you and learn from me, for I am gentle and humble in heart, and you will find rest for your souls. For my yoke is easy and my burden is light"—offer comfort and rest for those experiencing spiritual depression?

This passage reflects the heart of Jesus, offering a deeply personal invitation to those who feel spiritually weary and burdened. Spiritual depression often comes with feelings of heaviness, emptiness, and exhaustion, where connecting with God feels difficult and overwhelming. In this state, the call to "Come to me" reminds us that Jesus understands our struggles and desires to meet us where we are, offering rest and renewal.

The promise "I will give you rest" is profound. It's not a temporary or superficial relief but a deep, soul-refreshing rest that only Jesus can provide. Unlike worldly distractions that often leave us feeling more empty, His rest is restorative, renewing our spirit and reconnecting us with God's peace. Reflect on how this promise speaks to your own experiences of spiritual fatigue or despair. What does it mean to you to find rest in Jesus?

The imagery of taking on Jesus' yoke is particularly comforting for those weighed down by the burdens of spiritual depression. A yoke typically represents work or responsibility, yet Jesus describes His yoke as "easy" and His burden as "light." This doesn't mean that life's challenges disappear, but rather that Jesus walks alongside us, sharing the weight of our struggles. How does this image change your perspective on handling spiritual heaviness? How might relying on His strength instead of your own bring you peace?

Jesus also invites us to "learn from me, for I am gentle and humble in heart." This highlights His compassion and understanding. He doesn't approach us with condemnation or impatience but with gentleness, guiding us through our struggles with love and care. How does this understanding of Jesus' character encourage you to come to Him with your burdens, no matter how heavy they feel?

Finally, the phrase "you will find rest for your souls" emphasizes the spiritual renewal Jesus provides. When spiritual depression makes us feel disconnected or distant from God, this verse reassures us that rest and restoration are available when we turn to Him. What practical steps can you take to respond to His invitation, such as setting aside time for prayer, worship, or quiet reflection in His presence?

Matthew 11:28-30 reminds us that we don't have to navigate spiritual depression alone. How does embracing this promise of rest and renewal encourage you to trust Jesus with your struggles and find comfort in His presence? Reflect on how allowing Him to carry your burdens can lead to healing and a deeper relationship with Him.

Real-World Example:

Sophia had always been deeply committed to her faith, but after a series of difficult events, she began to feel overwhelmed and spiritually drained. Over the course of a year, she faced the loss of a close friend, mounting pressures at work, and increasing conflict within her family. She felt as though the weight of these struggles was crushing her. Despite attending church regularly and trying to maintain her spiritual disciplines, Sophia found herself feeling disconnected from God, questioning whether He truly cared about her burdens.

One Sunday, during a particularly low moment, Sophia's pastor preached on Matthew 11:28-30: "Come to me, all you who are weary and burdened, and I will give you rest." These words struck a chord in her heart, as if Jesus was speaking directly to her. She realized that while she had been trying to handle her struggles on her own, Jesus was inviting her to bring everything to Him.

That evening, Sophia sat quietly in her room with her Bible open to Matthew 11:28-30. For the first time in weeks, she prayed honestly, pouring out her pain, frustration, and weariness to God. She admitted that she didn't know how to fix her circumstances or even her own heart, but she asked Jesus to take the burdens she had been carrying. As she prayed, Sophia felt a small but significant sense of release, as if she was finally letting go of the weight that had been pressing on her.

Sophia decided to make this a daily practice. Each morning, she would begin her day with a simple prayer, offering her burdens to Jesus and asking for His strength to face whatever lay ahead. She also began meditating on Scriptures that reminded her of God's care, such as Psalm 46:1: "God is our refuge and strength, an ever-present help in trouble." She found comfort in the reminder that Jesus was not only willing but eager to share her load.

Over time, Sophia noticed a change in her perspective. While her circumstances hadn't immediately improved—work was still challenging, and family tensions persisted—she no longer felt crushed by them. She began to experience the "rest for your souls" that Jesus promised. Moments of peace and clarity replaced her previous sense of chaos, and she felt renewed strength to approach each day with hope.

Sophia also found that her renewed reliance on Jesus brought her closer to God. Worship felt meaningful again, and she began to sense His presence in small, everyday moments—a kind word from a colleague, a breakthrough in a family conversation, or even the beauty of nature during a morning walk. These reminders of God's faithfulness helped her to trust Him more deeply.

Through her journey, Sophia realized that Jesus' invitation wasn't just about removing burdens but about walking alongside her, providing strength and peace even in the midst of trials. Her story became a testimony to others in her church, showing that finding rest in Jesus is not about escaping life's difficulties but about allowing Him to carry you through them with His gentle and sustaining presence.

Small Prayer: Jesus, I come to You with my weariness and burdens. Please give me rest and refresh my soul. Amen.

Friday: Assurance of God's Unwavering Love

Explanation of Topic: This powerful assurance reminds us that nothing can separate us from God's love. It provides a firm foundation of hope and security, even in times of spiritual depression

Discussion Question: How can the assurance in Romans 8:38-39—"For I am convinced that neither death nor life, neither angels nor demons, neither the present nor the future, nor any powers, neither height nor depth, nor anything else in all creation, will be able to separate us from the love of God that is in Christ Jesus our Lord"—strengthen your faith and remind you of God's unwavering love during spiritual depression?

Spiritual depression often brings feelings of isolation and abandonment, as though God's presence and love have become distant or inaccessible. This passage directly counters those feelings, offering a powerful reminder that God's love is unshakable and unchanging, no matter our circumstances. Paul's bold declaration serves as a reassurance that nothing in creation, including our struggles, doubts, or failures, can separate us from God's love in Christ.

Reflect on the all-encompassing nature of Paul's list. He names extremes—life and death, angels and demons, the present and the future, height and depth—to emphasize that absolutely nothing is beyond the reach of God's love. How does this truth comfort you in moments when you feel distant from Him? What specific fears or doubts do you need to surrender to the assurance that God's love remains constant?

The mention of "the present nor the future" is particularly significant for those experiencing spiritual depression. Often, our present struggles feel overwhelming, and the uncertainty of the future amplifies our fears. This verse reminds us that God's love is not dependent on our current emotional state or our ability to feel His presence—it is rooted in His character and His promises. How can this knowledge encourage you to persevere in faith, even when emotions or circumstances make it difficult?

Consider how this passage challenges you to view your spiritual depression through the lens of God's eternal love. While the experience of depression may cause you to question your worth or God's attention to your pain, Romans 8:38-39 affirms that His love is greater than any internal or external force. How does knowing that His love is inseparable from you give you the courage to keep seeking Him, even in the darkest moments?

Practically, internalizing the truth of this passage might involve memorizing it, meditating on it during prayer, or writing it down as a reminder in moments of doubt. Reflect on how God's love, fully revealed through Jesus Christ, not only sustains you during spiritual depression but also serves as a foundation for renewed hope and faith. How can this assurance inspire you to trust God more deeply, knowing that His love is always with you, even when you struggle to sense it?

Real-World Example: Andrew, a dedicated believer, found himself in a deep spiritual crisis after experiencing a series of life-altering events. First, he lost his job unexpectedly, creating financial strain on his family. Shortly after, his closest friend moved across the country, leaving Andrew feeling isolated. To make matters worse, Andrew's father was diagnosed with a serious illness, and the weight of these challenges left him questioning God's presence in his life. Despite years of faith, Andrew began to feel spiritually dry and distant from God, as though his prayers were bouncing off the ceiling.

One evening, as he sat alone, consumed by doubt and despair, Andrew came across Romans 8:38-39: "For I am convinced that neither death nor life, neither angels nor demons, neither the present nor the future, nor any powers, neither height nor depth, nor anything else in all creation, will be able to separate us from the love of God that is in Christ Jesus our Lord." The words seemed to leap off the page, speaking directly to his situation. For the first time in weeks, Andrew felt a flicker of hope.

The passage reminded him that God's love wasn't dependent on his circumstances or feelings. It reassured him that even in his darkest moments, when he couldn't sense God's presence, God's love remained constant and unshakable. Andrew clung to this truth, repeating the verse aloud each morning as he began his day. Though his circumstances hadn't changed, this assurance gave him the strength to face them with renewed faith.

Andrew also began journaling his thoughts, reflecting on times in his past when he had clearly seen God's love and faithfulness. This exercise helped him to recognize that while he felt distant now, God's character hadn't changed. The same God who had carried him through past trials was with him in the present, even if it felt different.

He also reached out to his pastor, who encouraged him to continue immersing himself in Scriptures about God's love and to join a support group at his church. The group provided a safe space for Andrew to share his struggles and receive encouragement from others who had walked through similar spiritual crises. Hearing their stories of hope and restoration reminded Andrew that his current season of doubt didn't define his faith.

Over time, as Andrew meditated on Romans 8:38-39 and leaned on his faith community, he began to experience a sense of peace and reassurance. His circumstances didn't immediately improve—his father's health remained uncertain, and his job search was slow—but his perspective shifted. Instead of focusing on what was missing, he began to see evidence of God's love in small, daily blessings: a kind word from a stranger, an unexpected financial provision, or a moment of laughter with his children.

Andrew's journey showed him that God's love is not diminished by our circumstances or feelings. The assurance in Romans 8:38-39 became an anchor for his soul, helping him to weather the storm with renewed strength and hope. His story became a testimony to others, demonstrating that even in the midst of spiritual crises, nothing—not fear, failure, or uncertainty—can separate us from the love of God in Christ Jesus.

Small Prayer: Lord, thank You for Your unwavering love. Help me to remember that nothing can separate me from Your love, and give me strength to endure. Amen.

End of the Week Closing Prayer for Spiritual Depression

Heavenly Father,

We humbly come before You in the midst of our spiritual depression, acknowledging the heaviness in our hearts and the doubts that weigh us down. We seek Your comfort and peace, trusting that You are the God who draws near to the brokenhearted and saves those who are crushed in spirit. Though we may feel distant from You, we are reminded by Your Word that nothing can separate us from Your unfailing love and compassion.

Lord, strengthen our faith when it feels fragile and renew our trust in Your promises. Help us to remember that Your love is steadfast, Your mercies are new every morning, and Your faithfulness endures through all seasons. May we take refuge in the assurance that You walk with us through every valley, offering guidance, protection, and hope.

As we navigate this difficult season, teach us to find rest in Jesus, who invites us to lay our burdens at His feet. Refresh our souls with the presence of Your Spirit, and help us to lean into Your peace, which surpasses all understanding. Open our hearts to see glimpses of Your grace and provision in the midst of our struggles.

Surround us, Lord, with a supportive community of believers who can encourage, uplift, and walk alongside us on this journey. Grant us the courage to share our burdens with others and the humility to receive their love and prayers. Guide us toward healing and restoration, drawing us closer to You each step of the way.

Thank You for Your patience, Your compassion, and Your unchanging love. We place our hope in You, trusting that You will transform our sorrow into joy and our despair into renewed purpose. In the name of Jesus, our Savior and source of all peace, we pray.

Amen

Week 15: Spiritual Malnutrition

Introduction

Spiritual malnutrition refers to a state where an individual experiences reduced spiritual strength, impaired spiritual vision, and a diminished ability to digest spiritual food. Just as physical malnutrition affects the body, spiritual malnutrition affects our spiritual well-being, making it difficult to grow and thrive in our faith. The Bible offers guidance and nourishment for overcoming spiritual malnutrition and restoring spiritual health.

Definition

Spiritual Malnutrition: A condition characterized by reduced spiritual strength, impaired spiritual vision, and a diminished ability to digest spiritual food.

Key Scriptures

Matthew 4:4 (NIV)-"Jesus answered, 'It is written: Man shall not live on bread alone, but on every word that comes from the mouth of God. Spiritual nourishment comes from God's Word. Just as physical food sustains the body, God's Word sustains our spirit.

Hebrews 5:12-14 (NIV)-"In fact, though by this time you ought to be teachers, you need someone to teach you the elementary truths of God's word all over again. You need milk, not solid food! Anyone who lives on milk, being still an infant, is not acquainted with the teaching about righteousness. But solid food is for the mature, who by constant use have trained themselves to distinguish good from evil." This passage highlights the need for spiritual growth and maturity. Spiritual malnutrition occurs when we remain on "milk" and do not progress to "solid food."

Psalm 1:2-3 (NIV)-"But whose delight is in the law of the Lord, and who meditates on his law day and night. That person is like a tree planted by streams of water, which yields its fruit in season and whose leaf does not wither—whatever they do prospers. "Delighting in and meditating on God's Word provides spiritual nourishment and stability. Like a tree by water, we will flourish when we are rooted in Scripture.

John 6:35 (NIV)"Then Jesus declared, 'I am the bread of life. Whoever comes to me will never go hungry, and whoever believes in me will never be thirsty.'" Jesus is our spiritual sustenance. Coming to Him and believing in Him fulfills our deepest spiritual needs.

Colossians 3:16 (NIV)-"Let the message of Christ dwell among you richly as you teach and admonish one another with all wisdom through psalms, hymns, and songs from the Spirit, singing to God with gratitude in your hearts. "Allowing the message of Christ to dwell richly within us nourishes our spirits. Teaching and encouraging one another helps to combat spiritual malnutrition.

Monday: The Nourishment of God's Word

Explanation of Topic: God's Word sustains our spirit just as physical food sustains our body. Consistent intake of Scripture is essential for spiritual health and growth.

Discussion Question: How does God's Word provide spiritual nourishment, and how can you incorporate it more into your daily life? God's Word is described throughout Scripture as essential sustenance for the soul. Just as physical food nourishes and sustains the body, the Word of God feeds and strengthens our spirit. In Matthew 4:4, Jesus says, "Man shall not live on bread alone, but on every word that comes from the mouth of God," emphasizing that spiritual nourishment is as vital as physical sustenance. The Bible provides wisdom, encouragement, correction, and hope, equipping us to grow in faith, overcome challenges, and align our lives with God's purposes. How does viewing God's Word as essential nourishment change the way you approach it in your daily life? What steps can you take to make engaging with Scripture a consistent and meaningful practice? Reflect on how a deeper connection to God's

Word can refresh your spirit, provide clarity, and sustain you through all of life's seasons

Real-World Example: Rachel, a longtime believer, felt spiritually weak and distant from God after a year of overwhelming responsibilities. Quick to anger and easily discouraged, she longed for a deeper connection with God but didn't know how to restore her faith. One Sunday, her pastor's sermon on Matthew 4:4 struck her: just as the body needs food, the spirit needs regular nourishment from God's Word.

Determined to change, Rachel began dedicating 15 minutes each morning to Scripture and prayer, starting with the Psalms. As she immersed herself in God's Word, passages like Psalm 23 reassured her of God's guidance, and Philippians 4:13 became her anchor during stressful days. She also joined a small group Bible study, where she found encouragement and accountability.

Over time, Rachel's faith grew stronger. She became more patient, hopeful, and equipped to face challenges with trust in God. Scripture transformed from a routine task to a lifeline, reconnecting her with God's love and power. Her journey inspired others, showing how consistent time in God's Word brings renewal, strength, and spiritual growth.

Small Prayer: Lord, help me to seek nourishment from Your Word daily. Strengthen my spirit and guide my steps. Amen.

Tuesday: From Milk to Solid Food

Explanation of Topic: Spiritual growth requires moving from basic teachings to deeper understanding. This progression strengthens our faith and equips us to discern right from wrong.

Discussion Question: How does Hebrews 5:12-14—"In fact, though by this time you ought to be teachers, you need someone to teach you the elementary truths of God's word all over again. You need milk, not solid food! Anyone who lives on milk, being still an infant, is not acquainted with the teaching about righteousness. But solid food is for the mature, who by constant use have trained themselves to distinguish good from evil"—challenge you to move from spiritual "milk" to "solid food"? What steps can you take to grow in spiritual maturity?

This passage serves as both a critique and a call to action for believers. It highlights the importance of progressing in spiritual maturity, moving beyond the basics of the faith (spiritual "milk") to deeper understanding and application (spiritual "solid food"). The author of Hebrews urges believers to take ownership of their spiritual growth, recognizing that remaining at an immature level can hinder their ability to live out their faith effectively and discern God's will.

Spiritual "Milk" vs. "Solid Food":

The metaphor of "milk" represents the foundational teachings of the Christian faith—truths that are essential for new believers but not sufficient for long-term growth. "Solid food," on the other hand, signifies deeper understanding and application of God's Word, requiring intentional study, reflection, and practice. This distinction challenges us to assess where we are in our spiritual journey. Are we relying solely on the basics, or are we actively seeking to deepen our faith and knowledge?

The Call to Growth:

The passage suggests that spiritual maturity involves both learning and doing. The phrase "who by constant use have trained themselves to distinguish good from evil" emphasizes the importance of consistent practice and application of God's Word. Spiritual growth isn't automatic; it requires effort, discipline, and a willingness to engage with Scripture, prayer, and community in meaningful ways.

Self-Reflection:

Reflect on your own spiritual journey. Are there areas where you've remained at a surface level, relying on spiritual "milk"? What specific steps can you take to move toward "solid food"—a deeper understanding and application of God's truths? Consider the role of Bible study, prayer, accountability, and service in helping you grow.

Practical Steps to Spiritual Maturity:

1. **Intentional Bible Study:** Move beyond casual reading to in-depth study of Scripture. Use commentaries, study guides, or join a Bible study group to explore the deeper meanings and applications of God's Word.

2. **Prayerful Reflection:** Regularly ask God to reveal areas in your life where you need to grow and to help you apply His truths.

3. **Engage with Mature Believers:** Surround yourself with spiritually mature individuals who can mentor, challenge, and encourage you in your faith journey.

4. **Apply What You Learn:** Spiritual maturity isn't just about knowledge—it's about action. Look for ways to live out the principles you learn, such as serving others, sharing your faith, or making ethical decisions rooted in Scripture.

5. **Practice Discernment:** Actively seek to distinguish between what aligns with God's will and what doesn't, using Scripture as your guide.

Challenge to Action:

How does this passage motivate you to take steps toward spiritual maturity? What specific practices or disciplines can you incorporate into your daily life to ensure you're moving from "milk" to "solid food"? Reflect on the benefits of deeper spiritual growth—not only for your own faith but for your ability to teach, encourage, and disciple others in their journey.

Real-World Example: Michael had been a Christian for years, regularly attending church and small groups, but his faith felt stagnant. He realized he was relying on spiritual "milk," foundational teachings, rather than progressing to the "solid food" of deeper biblical truths. During a small group discussion on Hebrews 5:12-14, Michael felt challenged to grow in maturity and apply Scripture to life's complexities.

Motivated to change, he began studying the Bible deeply, using commentaries and focusing on books like Romans, which taught him about grace and sanctification. Michael joined a discipleship group to engage with advanced topics like apologetics and biblical ethics, pushing him to think critically and live out his faith. Mentoring a younger believer further deepened his understanding and compelled him to model his faith authentically.

Over time, Michael's spiritual life transformed. He developed wisdom and confidence to navigate moral dilemmas, reignited his prayer life, and found joy in applying God's Word. His journey illustrated the importance of moving beyond spiritual basics, inspiring others to pursue a deeper, more intentional relationship with God.

Small Prayer: Heavenly Father, guide me towards spiritual maturity. Help me to grow in understanding and apply Your teachings in my life. Amen.

Wednesday: Meditating on God's Word

Explanation of Topic: Delighting in and meditating on God's Word roots us deeply in His truth, providing spiritual nourishment and resilience.

Discussion Question: How does Psalm 1:2-3—"But whose delight is in the law of the Lord, and who meditates on his law day and night. That person is like a tree planted by streams of water, which yields its fruit in season and whose leaf does not wither—whatever they do prospers"— describe the benefits of delighting in and meditating on God's Word? How can this practice help you avoid spiritual malnutrition?

This passage offers a vivid image of the transformative power of consistently meditating on God's Word. Like a flourishing tree planted by streams of water, a believer who delights in Scripture draws nourishment, vitality, and strength from God. This spiritual sustenance leads to growth, resilience, and fruitfulness in their faith journey.

Real-World Example: Rebecca, a young professional, felt overwhelmed by a demanding job, strained friendships, and uncertainty about her future. Realizing her faith had taken a backseat, she joined a church small group, where Psalm 1:2-3 inspired her to prioritize God's Word.

She began spending 15 minutes daily meditating on Scripture, reflecting on passages like Philippians 4:6-7 and Romans 8:28, and journaling her thoughts. Applying these truths to her life, Rebecca found strength in Matthew 11:28-30 during stressful workdays and chose forgiveness using Ephesians 4:32 in conflicts. Over time, Rebecca's consistent engagement with Scripture transformed her. Like a tree planted by streams of water, she felt grounded, less anxious, and more resilient. Her relationships improved, and she faced challenges with calm and hope. Rebecca's story became an inspiration to others, demonstrating that prioritizing God's Word brings stability and spiritual growth in every area of life.

Small Prayer: Lord, may Your Word be my delight and meditation day and night. Nourish my soul and help me to flourish like a tree by streams of water. Amen.

Thursday: Jesus, the Bread of Life

Explanation of Topic: Jesus is our ultimate spiritual sustenance. Building a deeper relationship with Him fulfills our spiritual hunger and thirst.

Discussion Question: How does Jesus, as the bread of life, fulfill our spiritual hunger as described in John 6:35—"Then Jesus declared, 'I am the bread of life. Whoever comes to me will never go hungry, and whoever believes in me will never be thirsty'"? How can you deepen your relationship with Him to experience this fulfillment?

In this profound declaration, Jesus identifies Himself as the ultimate source of spiritual nourishment and satisfaction. Bread, a staple food in many cultures, represents sustenance and life. By calling Himself the bread of life, Jesus emphasizes that He is essential for our spiritual well-being, offering what nothing else in the world can provide—a deep, enduring fulfillment for our soul's hunger.

Fulfilling Our Spiritual Hunger:

1. **Satisfying the Deepest Longings:** Just as physical hunger signals our body's need for sustenance, spiritual hunger reflects our soul's longing for connection with God. Jesus promises that those who come to Him and believe in Him will never experience spiritual emptiness. Reflect on how seeking fulfillment in worldly pursuits—such as success, possessions, or relationships—often leaves us unsatisfied, while turning to Jesus provides lasting peace and joy.

2. **Eternal Life and Purpose:** Jesus not only sustains us in the present but offers eternal life to those who believe in Him. This truth redefines our purpose, anchoring our lives in His grace and promises rather than fleeting goals or achievements.

3. **Ongoing Sustenance:** The phrase "never go hungry" suggests that Jesus provides continual nourishment, meeting our daily spiritual needs. His presence and Word strengthen us to navigate life's challenges, offering wisdom, comfort, and hope.

Deepening Your Relationship with Jesus:

To fully experience the fulfillment Jesus offers, we must actively cultivate our relationship with Him. Consider these practical steps:

1. **Consistent Prayer:** Spend time in heartfelt conversation with Jesus, sharing your thoughts, struggles, and gratitude. Prayer nurtures intimacy and aligns your heart with His will.

2. **Feeding on His Word:** Regularly read and meditate on Scripture, allowing His teachings to guide your actions and decisions.

3. **Worship:** Engage in personal and communal worship to focus on His character and express your devotion.

4. **Service and Obedience:** Live out your faith by serving others and following His commands, reflecting His love to the world.

5. **Trust and Surrender:** Actively rely on Jesus in both joyful and challenging seasons, trusting that He is enough to meet all your needs.

Self-Reflection:

- How does the image of Jesus as the bread of life resonate with your own experiences of spiritual hunger?

- Are there areas in your life where you've sought fulfillment apart from Him? How can you redirect your focus to find true satisfaction in Christ?

- What practical steps can you take to deepen your relationship with Him, ensuring that you regularly receive the spiritual nourishment He provides?

By coming to Jesus daily, we experience the fullness of His presence and the abundant life He promises. Reflect on how embracing Him as the bread of life can transform not only your spiritual hunger but also your outlook, priorities, and purpose, leading to a life of deeper faith, joy, and peace.

Real-World Example: Samantha had always considered herself a believer, faithfully attending church and participating in her small group. However, she often felt a lingering sense of emptiness, even after spiritual activities. Her daily life was filled with striving—working hard to achieve professional success, maintaining her relationships, and trying to meet everyone's expectations. Despite her accomplishments, Samantha couldn't shake the feeling that something was missing. She frequently sought validation from others and found herself exhausted by the pressure to keep up appearances.

One Sunday, her pastor preached on John 6:35: "I am the bread of life. Whoever comes to me will never go hungry, and whoever believes in me will never be thirsty." The message struck Samantha deeply. She realized that while she knew about Jesus, she hadn't been seeking Him as the source of her satisfaction. She had been trying to fill her spiritual hunger with achievements, approval, and even her church involvement, but none of it truly satisfied her soul.

Determined to experience the fulfillment Jesus promised, Samantha decided to focus on deepening her personal relationship with Him. She began setting aside quiet time each morning to pray and meditate on Scripture. Initially, it felt difficult—her mind often wandered to her to-do list or her worries. But as she persisted, Samantha started to experience a profound sense of peace during these moments with Jesus. Passages like Psalm 23:1—"The Lord is my shepherd; I lack nothing"—reminded her that Jesus was enough to meet all her needs.

Samantha also committed to journaling her thoughts and prayers, honestly expressing her struggles and asking Jesus to fill the void she felt. This practice helped her uncover areas where she had been relying on external validation instead of trusting in God's unconditional love. She began to internalize verses like Romans 8:38-39, which assured her that nothing could separate her from God's love.

In addition to personal prayer and Bible study, Samantha sought community with other believers who were passionate about their faith. She joined a discipleship group that focused on cultivating a deeper relationship with Jesus. Hearing how others had found fulfillment in Christ inspired Samantha to continue pursuing Him with her whole heart.

Over time, Samantha noticed a significant shift in her life. The things that once consumed her—career success, social approval, and perfectionism—no longer held the same power over her. Instead, she found joy in the simple yet profound reality of knowing Jesus intimately. She felt less anxious and more at peace, knowing that her worth wasn't tied to what she accomplished but to her identity as a child of God.

When challenges arose, Samantha turned to Jesus as her source of strength and sustenance. She memorized Scriptures like Matthew 11:28-30, reminding herself to lay her burdens at His feet and trust in His provision. Her relationship with Jesus became the foundation of her life, giving her a sense of fulfillment and purpose that nothing else could offer.

Samantha's journey of finding satisfaction in Jesus transformed not only her spiritual life but also her relationships and outlook on the future. By making Jesus the bread of life in her daily walk, she experienced the abundant life He promises—a life rooted in peace, joy, and the assurance of His unwavering presence. Her story became a testimony to others, showing that true fulfillment is found not in the things of this world but in a deep, personal relationship with Christ.

Small Prayer: Jesus, You are the bread of life. Fill my heart with Your presence and satisfy my deepest needs. Amen.

Friday: The Richness of Christ's Message

Explanation of Topic: Allowing the message of Christ to dwell richly within us and supporting one another in faith combats spiritual malnutrition and strengthens the body of Christ.

Discussion Question: How does Colossians 3:16—"Let the message of Christ dwell among you richly as you teach and admonish one another with all wisdom through psalms, hymns, and songs from the Spirit, singing to God with gratitude in your hearts"—encourage us to nourish our spirits and support one another in our faith journey?

This verse highlights the importance of allowing the message of Christ—the truth of His Word and teachings—to deeply influence and shape our lives. The word "dwell" suggests a constant, abiding presence of Christ's message in our hearts and minds, indicating that nourishing our spirits requires consistent engagement with His Word. Additionally, the verse emphasizes the role of community, urging believers to teach, admonish, and encourage one another as part of their spiritual growth.

Nourishing Our Spirits:

1. **Letting Christ's Word Dwell Richly:** To nourish our spirits, we must not merely read Scripture superficially but allow it to penetrate our hearts and transform our thinking. This means

meditating on God's Word, applying it to our lives, and letting it guide our decisions and attitudes. When Christ's message dwells richly within us, it serves as a source of wisdom, peace, and encouragement, equipping us to face life's challenges with faith and strength.

2. **Worship as Spiritual Nourishment:** The verse mentions "psalms, hymns, and songs from the Spirit" as a means of expressing gratitude and connecting with God. Worship, whether through music, prayer, or other forms, renews our spirits and reminds us of God's presence and faithfulness.

Supporting One Another:

1. **Teaching and Admonishing:** This verse emphasizes the communal aspect of faith, where believers are called to teach and guide each other with wisdom. Sharing insights from Scripture, offering encouragement, and gently correcting one another when needed fosters spiritual growth and accountability within the body of Christ.

2. **Encouragement through Gratitude and Worship:** When we express gratitude and worship together, we build each other up and create a sense of unity. Celebrating God's goodness as a community strengthens our collective faith and helps us remain focused on His promises.

Reflection:

- How does this verse challenge you to make the message of Christ a central part of your daily life? Are there specific practices—such as prayer, Bible study, or worship—that you can prioritize to allow His Word to dwell more richly within you?

- In what ways have you experienced the encouragement and wisdom of fellow believers in your faith journey? How can you actively contribute to the spiritual nourishment of others?

Practical Application:

1. **Personal Engagement with Scripture:** Commit to a daily habit of reading and meditating on God's Word. Reflect on how its truths can guide your thoughts, decisions, and interactions.

2. **Participate in Community Worship:** Join a small group or church gathering where worship and gratitude are central, allowing the collective faith of others to inspire and strengthen your own.

3. **Encourage and Teach Others:** Look for opportunities to share what you've learned from Scripture with someone who may need encouragement or wisdom. Offer to pray with or for them, reinforcing the sense of community and shared growth.

Challenge to Action:

How can you create a rhythm in your life where the message of Christ dwells richly and consistently? What steps can you take to both nourish your own spirit and support the faith journey of those around you? Reflect on how this practice can transform not only your relationship with God but also the relationships within your community of faith, as you grow together in wisdom, gratitude, and worship.

Real-World Example:

At Hope Community Church, the congregation was known for its vibrant focus on living out Colossians 3:16. Their commitment to teaching and encouraging one another through worship, study, and fellowship created a spiritually nourishing environment that profoundly impacted its members and the surrounding community.

Teaching Through God's Word:

Hope Community Church placed a strong emphasis on Scripture as the foundation of its ministry. Every Sunday, the pastor delivered sermons deeply rooted in biblical teaching, often connecting Scripture to real-life challenges. For example, during a sermon series on trusting God, the pastor explored Proverbs 3:5-6, encouraging members to share personal stories about how they had relied on God in uncertain times. These testimonies were compiled into a booklet, which became a source of encouragement for the congregation.

The church also offered a variety of Bible study groups tailored to different age groups and life stages. One group for young adults delved into Ephesians 4:1-3 to discuss unity and forgiveness. During a session, a member named James shared how he reconciled with a friend after years of estrangement, inspired by the study's teachings. His story encouraged others in the group to reflect on their relationships and seek reconciliation where needed.

To make biblical learning accessible, the church created an app where members could access sermon notes, daily devotionals, and a "Question of the Week" section that tackled common faith-related challenges. For instance, one week's topic was "How do I discern God's will?" Members engaged in discussions online, sharing insights and encouraging one another.

Encouraging Through Worship:

Worship at Hope Community Church was designed to be both uplifting and deeply rooted in Scripture. The worship team carefully selected songs that complemented the week's teaching, blending contemporary worship music with traditional hymns. For instance, after a sermon on Psalm 23, the congregation sang "Shepherd of My Soul" and "Great Is Thy Faithfulness." These songs reinforced the message, helping members internalize biblical truths through music.

The church also hosted quarterly worship nights that featured extended times of singing, prayer, and Scripture reading. These evenings became a space for members to pour out their hearts to God, express gratitude, and intercede for one another. During one worship night, a member named Lisa, who had been battling anxiety, shared how the song "It Is Well With My Soul" reminded her of God's sovereignty and brought her peace.

Fostering Fellowship:

Hope Community Church understood that true spiritual growth often happens in the context of relationships. They prioritized creating opportunities for members to connect beyond Sunday services. Monthly fellowship dinners brought together families, singles, and seniors, encouraging conversations and deeper relationships. At one dinner, a widower named Tom shared how the church's community had become his family after the loss of his wife, demonstrating the power of fellowship in healing and support.

Small groups were another cornerstone of the church's community life. Each group included time for Bible study, prayer, and sharing personal experiences. One group for young mothers focused on Philippians 4:13 during a study on finding strength in Christ. Members supported one another through the challenges of parenting, often providing meals, babysitting, or simply a listening ear.

Additionally, the church organized service projects that allowed members to live out their faith together. During one project, members came together to renovate a local shelter. As they painted walls and built furniture, they shared stories of how serving others deepened their understanding of Matthew 25:40: "Whatever you did for one of the least of these brothers and sisters of mine, you did for me."

Transformational Impact:

The focus on worship, study, and fellowship transformed the lives of individuals and the church as a whole. Members like Sarah, who initially joined the church feeling spiritually disconnected, found renewed faith through the consistent teaching and encouragement of her small group. Meanwhile, the youth group organized worship nights at a local park, drawing dozens of teens from the community who were curious about their vibrant faith.

Through its commitment to living out Colossians 3:16, Hope Community Church became a thriving hub of spiritual growth, encouragement, and love. Members not only grew closer to God but also to one another, creating a ripple effect of unity and faith that reached far beyond the church walls. Their example demonstrated that when a church community is grounded in teaching, worship, and fellowship, it becomes a powerful force for transformation and hope

Small Prayer: Heavenly Father, let the message of Christ dwell richly within me. Help me to teach, admonish, and encourage others in their faith journey. Amen.

End of the Week Closing Prayer for Spiritual Malnutrition

Heavenly Father,

We humbly come before You, acknowledging how much we need Your spiritual nourishment and guidance every day. You are the source of all wisdom, strength, and peace, and we thank You for offering us the Bread of Life through Your Son, Jesus Christ. Without You, we are empty, but in You, we find fulfillment, purpose, and joy.

Lord, help us to seek Your Word daily—not out of obligation, but with hearts eager to know You more deeply. Teach us to meditate on Your truths and let them take root in our lives, transforming our thoughts, attitudes, and actions. May Your Word be a lamp to our feet and a light for our path, guiding us through every challenge and decision.

Father, we ask for growth in spiritual maturity. Move us beyond surface-level faith to a deep and abiding relationship with You. Strengthen our faith so that we may stand firm in times of doubt, difficulty, or temptation. Show us how to apply Your teachings in practical ways, making a tangible impact in our lives and the lives of those around us.

Surround us, Lord, with a community of believers who will encourage, support, and challenge us in our spiritual journey. May we also be sources of encouragement to others, sharing Your love and truth through our words and actions. Let our fellowship be marked by unity, grace, and a shared commitment to glorify You.

Thank You, Father, for being our Bread of Life. Thank You for meeting our deepest spiritual needs, for filling the emptiness within us, and for drawing us closer to You. Your faithfulness sustains us, Your Word revives us, and Your Spirit renews us.

As we move forward, may we continually hunger and thirst for Your righteousness, finding satisfaction in Your presence. May we live each day with hearts full of gratitude for all You've done and with lives that reflect Your glory.

We lift this prayer in the name of Jesus, our Savior and sustainer, who provides for us in ways beyond what we can imagine.

Amen.

Conclusion of the 15-Week Study Guide

Congratulations!

Congratulations on completing this 15-week study guide on spiritual ailments! Over the past weeks, you have taken an incredible journey of faith, addressing challenges that can hinder spiritual growth and exploring the powerful truths found in God's Word to overcome them.

As we reflect on this journey, we are reminded of how Scripture provides guidance, comfort, and strength in every season of life. Together, we have learned to trust in God's promises, lean on His unchanging character, and embrace the support of a faith-filled community. Most importantly, we have deepened our relationship with Him, discovering how His presence sustains and transforms us.

As you conclude this study, let these lessons become a foundation for your spiritual walk. Carry them with you, applying them in your daily life, and remaining vigilant in your pursuit of God's presence and guidance. Know that this is not the end but a stepping stone toward greater spiritual maturity and intimacy with Him.

Thank you for committing to this journey. Your dedication and openness to grow in your faith are an inspiration. May you continue to seek His wisdom, walk in His ways, and live out His truth, shining His light in the world around you.

With gratitude and blessings,

Brooklyn Hector

Closing Prayer

Heavenly Father, we thank You for guiding us through this study. Thank You for revealing the areas in our lives that need Your healing touch. As we move forward, help us to remember and apply the lessons we've learned. Strengthen our faith, renew our spirits, and keep us close to You. May we continue to grow in our relationship with You and reflect Your love in all we do. In Jesus' name, Amen.Congratulations on completing the 15-week study guide on spiritual ailments. Over the past weeks, we have tackled various challenges that can hinder our spiritual growth and discovered powerful biblical insights to address them.

Reflecting on this journey, we have seen how God's Word provides guidance, comfort, and strength. We have learned to lean on His promises, find support in our community, and cultivate a deeper relationship with Him.

As we conclude this study, let's carry forward the lessons we've learned and continue to apply them in our daily lives. May we remain vigilant in our spiritual walk, always seeking God's presence and guidance.

www.ingramcontent.com/pod-product-compliance
Lightning Source LLC
Chambersburg PA
CBHW051201120626
46547CB00012B/1149